The Pocket Guide

Travel Book Series

ISBN 1-86500-830 3
1. Title: The Pocket Guide to The Pilbara
Book Design: David Kirkland
Text: David Kirkland
Photography: David Kirkland. (www.kirklandphotos.com)
Scanning: Christina and Tim Nemeth, TT Digital
Illustration: Malcolm Lindsay

First printed March 2000
Second Edition May 2002
Third Edition June 2005

Published by Hema Maps Pty Ltd
PO Box 4365, Eight Mile Plains
Brisbane, Queensland, Australia 4113
Phone: 61 7 3340 0000
Fax: 61 7 3340 0099
E-Mail: manager@hemamaps.com.au
Web: www.hemamaps.com

# The Pocket Guide to The Pilbara

by
David Kirkland

# THE PILBARA

**Location:** The Pilbara is located about 1,600 kilometres north of Perth, the capital of Western Australia.

**Size:** The region covers roughly 500,000 square kilometres and is bordered by the Gascoyne Region in the south, the Kimberley Region in the north, the Indian Ocean to the west and the Northern Territory border to the east.

**Population:** The Pilbara has a population of about 50,000.

**Primary centres a**re located in Karratha and Port Hedland on the coast and Tom Price and Newman inland.

**Air access:** Regular air access is provided to each of the primary centres.

**Road access:** The Pilbara has two major road arteries: The North West Coastal Highway and the Great Northern Highway, which passes through Newman.

# Acknowledgements

I'd like to acknowledge the following people for their assistance in the making of this book: **Vaughan Sutherland,** for the many distinctive creative elements used in this publication, and his entrepreneurial flair which was a constant source of encouragement; Pilbara Tourism Association chairman **Ian Laurance,** for his guidance and support, and the board members of the association (particularly Heather, who appears with me in the fantastic photograph taken by **Simon Westlake** on page 10). I'd like to thank **Bill, Terry and Eddie,** of Tourism Co-ordinates, for their assistance during my tenure, **Kirsty Hunt** for her youthful exuberance and **Rob Standaloft** for his "constant instruction", but particularly for their friendship. I'd also like to thank each of the region's tourist bureau managers and my replacement, **Stephen Pahl,** all of whom continue to tirelessly promote the region. And finally, I'd like to thank the operators involved in the Pilbara's tourism industry for sharing with me their belief in the potential of this vast and fascinating part of the world to become a premier adventure destination.

To each of you, my sincere thanks.

To my son, Daniel

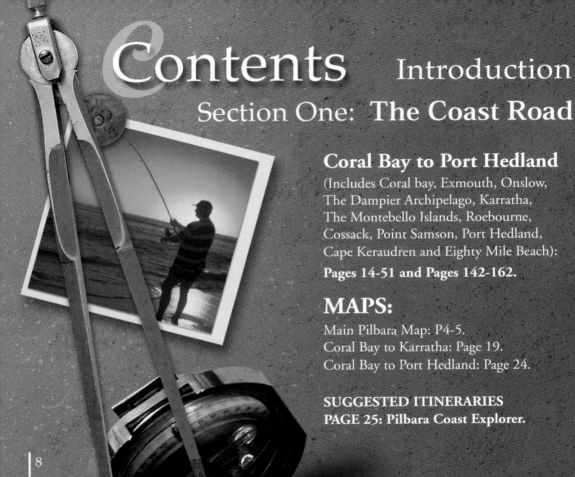

# Contents

## Introduction

## Section One:  The Coast Road

### Coral Bay to Port Hedland

(Includes Coral bay, Exmouth, Onslow,
The Dampier Archipelago, Karratha,
The Montebello Islands, Roebourne,
Cossack, Point Samson, Port Hedland,
Cape Keraudren and Eighty Mile Beach):

## MAPS:

# Section Two: The Inland Road

## Coral Bay to Port Hedland via Karijini

(Includes Python Pool, Millstream Station, Karijini National Park,
Mt Bruce, Tom Price, Newman, The Western Desert,
Nullagine, Marble Bar and Coppins Gap):

## MAPS:

### SUGGESTED ITINERARIES

So you're visiting the Pilbara and you want to know what there is to see and do. Time, money and interest are all likely to make you selective but the last thing you want to feel at the end of your visit is that you've missed anything.

Well, I'd like to think you've come to the right book!

I should point out from the outset that this book is not meant to be a definitive guide to the Pilbara (it's pocket status is an accurate reflection of the depths to which I have plunged on any single subject). In short, it's the sort of book I wish had been available when I arrived in the Pilbara -- plenty of photographs to help me decide where to go, interesting insights, a balanced reference to the best places to visit and helpful information presented in a way that would keep the attention of a wandering mind with a low tolerance for rambling prose.

Within its covers, you'll find information gathered during my two years as head of the Pilbara region's tourism authority. Having travelled more than 100,000 km in search of the best places in the Pilbara, pored over countless reference books and spent innumerable mornings crouched over my camera hoping to catch the region in its best light, I'd like to think I have a better idea than most about what the Pilbara has to offer the traveller...

But before I go on, let me get a few things out of the way: Yes, the Pilbara is hot, uncomfortably so from December to March when you can literally fry an egg on the bitumen, and yes, during some months of the year it has flies that could gnaw out the insides of your eye sockets given half a chance. It's also true that after a good day of driving with your windows down your hair will be as soft as concrete from the red dust, and yes, the Pilbara can be dangerous. It's remote and unpredictable and poor planning will see you sharing the same fate as some of the nation's most intrepid explorers.

But having got that out of the way, let me assure you, if it's adventure and a remote frontier experience you're looking for, you've come to the right place. Indulge me for a minute while I slip back into some of the promotional material I've written on the region in the past:

*"Picture yourself wandering through a 40,000 year old gallery of ancient Aboriginal rock engravings or descending a kilometre along winding gorges that have been carved into one of the oldest landscapes on earth (two and a half billion years old!). Imagine joining a four wheel drive expedition along the edge of the Great Sandy Desert or tracing the famous Canning Stock Route and following in the footsteps of some of the country's great explorers. Wander the ancient riverbeds of Karijini National Park with its spectacular subterranean pools, or shower under one of its many waterfalls. Visit Millstream Station, part of the Millstream Chichester National Park, a palm-fringed oasis well known to the Afghan cameleers of the Pilbara's pioneering past, or journey out to the Rudall River National Park where the landscape has been virtually unchanged since the beginning of time. And, if you're into beaches and ocean, cast your footsteps in the hundreds of kilometres of*

*pristine coastline that borders the Pilbara, swim alongside massive whale sharks off the Ningaloo Reef (The West Coast's Great Barrier Reef), hire a boat, snorkel or simply lose yourself among the 200 virgin islands that lie off the Pilbara coast..."*

Sounds inviting, huh? Well, now you're starting to get a taste for the Pilbara.

For those planning to visit the region, this book will be a good introduction and, I hope, a valuable guide, particularly for those looking to understand a bit more about the land that surrounds them, and those who are chasing some "soft adventure" (ie take me to the highlights but tuck me in at night).

In summary, there is so much to see and do in the Pilbara that, after two years, I think I've only scratched the surface. As a photographer I can say the Pilbara is not a single photograph, it's an experience, and that the many images in this book are a pale reflection of what you see when you are actually there. As a writer I can say that there is much about the Pilbara that I have not been able to put into words -- a feeling, a sense, something you can only appreciate when, for example, you're standing on the fringe of the Great Sandy Desert surrounded only by distant horizons and listening to the sounds of the earth. And as a person who has had the good fortune to be able to travel this region widely, I can only encourage you to take your time and look beyond your first impression.

The Pilbara is one of the oldest land masses in the world and there is much to be enjoyed and learned by coming here. If you take the time to look and listen, I'm sure you won't be disappointed.

# Ningaloo Reef

## Including Coral Bay, Exmouth and Onslow

Ningaloo Reef is Western Australia's Great Barrier Reef, and it's well worth the few hours deviation off the coastal highway. The settings provided in Cape Range National Park, which borders the reef, are stunning (there's a good reason why some of the world's largest hotel chains have been trying so hard to get their toes in the water). Turquoise waters, pristine, white sandy beaches, prolific marine life - dugongs, manta rays, whales and whale sharks (between March and June) and some very accessible reef snorkelling ( just park your car, don the mask and wander into the water). Add to that diving, fishing, sea kayaking, surfing and some great little picnic and camping spots, and you're bound to find something to keep you there longer. In my opinion though, what makes the Ningaloo Reef most appealing - regardless of the direction you're going - is the contrast between it and the inland Pilbara. In particular, it's the extremes in colour and landscapes -- the contrast of the coastline's white sand and its clear blue waters against the dry, red inland landscape and its brackish waterholes. If it's contrasting experiences you're after, you'd be doing yourself a huge disservice if you didn't make every effort to see as much as you can of both while you're visiting the north-west.

**Previous Page:** Sunset fishing is a popular pastime along the beaches near Exmouth.
**Above:** Vlamingh Lighthouse, Exmouth.
**Right**: Swimming with the whale sharks is a big drawcard to Ningaloo Reef.

# The Whale Sharks
### (Rhincodon typus)

I would love to tell you that swimming with the whale sharks was the highlight of my time in Western Australia, but it was never to be. On the occasions I turned up at Exmouth or Coral Bay with goggles and snorkels in hand, I was joined by @@@##!!! cyclone-like conditions or it was off season (outside of March and June). The experience, however, remains one of my life's ambitions. For those who are likely to succeed where I didn't, here's some preliminary info. At up to 18m (60ft) in length, the whale shark is the biggest fish in the ocean and the biggest cold blooded animal in the world. Thankfully, it eats only plankton (it would make for an interesting adaptation of 'Jaws' if they didn't) and up to 40 on one day have been spotted cruising the reef. The process involved in seeing the whale sharks is simple if you're looking to do a tour out of Coral Bay or Exmouth. A spotter plane flies out and locates the whale shark/s and you all jump on a boat which drops you just ahead of where the shark is likely to pass. It slowly cruises by doing its giant vacuum cleaner act of eating tiny sea particles, and you paddle alongside.

Fantastic. I could kick myself for missing it!

And if you're like me and arrive outside of whale shark season, don't be too discouraged as there's still heaps to see underwater .......like the Manta Rays (Pictured).

For more information about "The one that got away" contact The Exmouth Tourist Bureau.

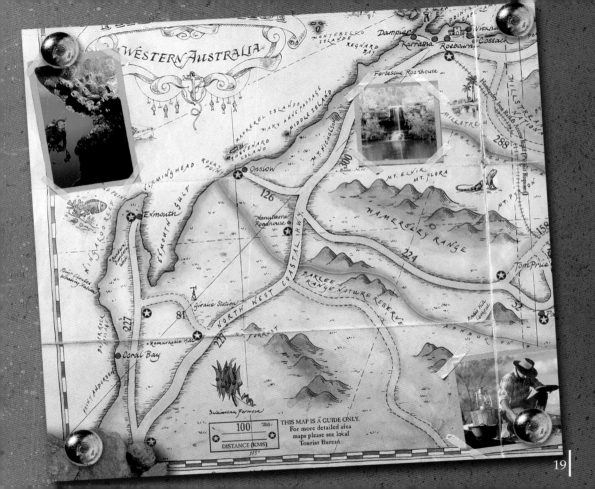

WESTERN AUSTRALIA

Dampier
Karratha
Roebourne
Cossack

Montebello Islands
Regnard Bay

Fortescue Roadhouse

Millstream National

Mackerel Islands
Mary Anne Passage
Middle Island
Thevenard Island

Flaming Head
Rocky Point

Onslow

Mt Nicholson

288

Mt Elvir
Mt Flora

300

126

HAMERSLEY RANGE

Exmouth

Nanutarra Roadhouse

Ningaloo Reef

Yardie Creek

224

Tom Price

Giralia Station

BARLEE RANGE NATURE RESERVE

NORTH WEST COASTAL HWY

32

227

81

Remarkable Hill

Coral Bay

FORREST

ASHBURTON

Solanum Formosa

100

DISTANCE (KMS)

THIS MAP IS A GUIDE ONLY.
For more detailed area
maps please see local
Tourist Bureau

**Coral Bay to Exmouth:** If you put Coral Bay anywhere near a capital city, it would become as popular as Noosa in Queensland or Byron Bay in NSW. It's an idyllic retreat - a small community, a beautiful outlook over the yacht moored bay - fine white sand bordered by towering dunes, clear water, temperate weather and easy access to the reef. So far, its remoteness has limited development and, hopefully, it will stay that way... though I doubt it.

One of the most pleasurable trips I have experienced in Western Australia lies along the coastline between Coral Bay and Exmouth. A four wheel drive helps, though the only real tricky bit - assuming good weather - is getting across Yardie Creek on high tide. You'll need to get directions (one of the information centres or a national park office should help) as signage is scant. Of course it's well patronised by those who know it - the fishermen and the locals - and I'd hate to try the narrow tracks that border the dunes in peak season but, outside of that, believe me - it's well worth it. There are some stunning views from designated camping spots and picnic areas between the dunes and, again, the reef is so accessible. There's also the Dugong Sanctuary and, if you're travelling from the south, you'll come out at the base of the Ningaloo Marine Park which should be one of the reasons you're this far north anyway. **Quick Tip:** Personally, I'd plan for at least a night in Coral Bay and a night in Exmouth with a camp out in between. And if you have a sea kayak or boat, bring it!

**Left:** A fisherman's dream. **Right:** Turquoise Bay -- it doesn't get much better than this!

# Onslow

Onslow's claim to fame, apart from being a sleepy fishing community and a gateway to Ningaloo Reef and the increasingly popular Mackerel Islands, is the fact it was bombed by the Japanese in the Second World War. It used to be a submarine base. From the lookout you can still see the huge refuelling tanks.

It's a fair way off the beaten track (assuming you're heading somewhere else) which, in itself, can be an attraction and the people are friendly in a casual sort of way.

Apart from fishing, there's a large Aboriginal community which - at least when I was there - produced some interesting art and artifacts (which were invariably making their way to Karijini to sell to the tourists).

If you haven't seen termite mounds before, the plain (photo) separating Onslow from the main highway has an abundance of them, which makes for a pretty good picture, methinks.

# SUGGESTED ITINERARY
## Pilbara Coast Explorer

**Ningaloo Reef - Onslow - Karratha - Dampier - Cossack - Point Samson - Port Hedland - 80 Mile Beach**
(allow five days)

After snorkelling and diving on the Ningaloo Reef, head north along the North West Coastal Highway before turning west through the termite mound covered landscape to the fishing community of Onslow. Heading further north, Karratha is a great base to explore the Dampier Archipelago, drop in to the North-West Shelf Gas Project Visitors' Centre or lose yourself among the 42 islands of the coast. Next stop is the historic towns of Roebourne and Cossack and a laid-back visit to Point Samson before the drive further north to Port Hedland where you'll see trains up to three kilometres long and massive ships carrying iron ore . Continuing up the North-West Coastal highway, pull in at Cape Keraudren, the start of 80 Mile Beach, and sit back to enjoy one of the most remote and expansive stretches of beach in Australia.

**Highlights:** Ningaloo Reef, the beaches, fishing, remote islands and an insight into Australia's natural gas resource industry.

**Below:** Overlooking Cape Range National Park.

# Karratha

Including the Dampier Archipelago,
Roebourne, Cossack and Point Samson

*K*arratha (an Aboriginal word for "Good Country") is the administrative centre for the Pilbara and a good place to base yourself to explore the surrounding area. It has the largest shopping centre in the north-west and a range of accommodation (though you need to be quick, as demand tends to exceed supply due to the area's massive resource boom). Me, I'd ring ahead (the Karratha Tourist Bureau does bookings) to make sure I had somewhere to stay for a night. then I'd plan to spend a couple of days either side checking out the Aboriginal engravings at Deep Gorge on the Burrup Peninsula as well as the Woodside Visitors Centre for an insight into the massive natural gas project. Other options include a fishing trip, a tour of the huge salt lakes, a boat trip out among the Dampier Archipelago's 42 islands or, if you're around at the right time of year, a trip out to the Montebello Islands. If you're doing the old "low budget camping trip of the north-west", at very least, Karratha is a good place to grab a shower, do the washing and replenish camping stocks before heading back out.

Dampier Archipelago

# ROCK OF AGES

Kangaroos, emus, turtles, boomerangs and mythological figures are what you'll find in abundance out on the Burrup Peninsula -- the most prolific aboriginal rock engraving site in the world (more than 500,000 engravings recorded). A wander through the rubble-strewn valleys of the peninsula is an excursion into an ancient art gallery. On either side of you, pecked into the rock, are hundreds of works of art from a 40,000 year-old culture -- time capsules from a distant past.

Deep Gorge is one of the most accessible valleys, out towards Hearson's Cove (refer page 33). Literally hundreds of engravings cover the rocks. While most of them seem representational of animals and weapons, interpretative stories abound, and with a good imagination you can see spacemen and maybe even the first white settler to come into contact with Aboriginal people. It's a leisurely walk up the valley and, while many of the engravings are obvious, it's fascinating to just sit down and allow your eyes to adjust - a change of light, a different angle can reveal an engraving you previously didn't realise was there.

Quite obviously, the valley was a special meeting place for Aboriginal people, who have left a rich, artistic heritage which has survived thousands of years. Let's all make sure it's still there for others to see thousands of years from now.

The Burrup Peninsula is the most concentrated rock art site in the world, followed by Toro Moerto on the Rio Majes in Peru.

**Above:** Not a bad day's catch in the Dampier Archipelago.

# Driving around Karratha

## Option 1: Hamersley Iron Tour, Woodside Visitors Centre, Hearson's Cove, Aboriginal rock art

Take a half hour drive to the Hamersley Training Centre to arrive at 9am and do a two hour tour of the company's huge iron operations. Tour includes bus ride, talk and a video (to watch not keep). You'll need to pay a nominal fee for a ticket from the Karratha Information Bureau the day before. Catch a look at the big ships being loaded with iron ore and look out over the 42 islands that make up the Dampier Archipelago. There's also a tour of the salt operation if you're interested. Then jump in your car and head out to Dampier for a bite to eat on the waterfront. On your way back to Karratha, turn out onto the Burrup Peninsula and drop in at the Woodside Visitor's Centre for a fascinating insight into the North-West Shelf Gas Project (allow about 45 minutes). Heading back in your car, follow the sign along the unsealed road to Hearson's Cove for a bit of a paddle. It's a popular swimming site for the locals (though make sure you pick the tide if you want it to look like the postcards). Hit your odometer when you leave Hearson's Cove and travel 1.1 kilometres back before taking a turn on your left and going about 100 metres to

Deep Gorge - one of the most prolific Aboriginal engraving sites in the world. Wander among the huge iron encrusted boulders that form this ancient art gallery and pick out the various shapes which have been etched into the rock.

Self Driv
Tour

Hamersley Iron,
Woodside Visito
Centre,
Hearson's C
Aborigi

## Option Two:
### Roebourne, Cossack, Point Samson.

You'll need to be prepared to travel about 100 km round trip. Leave Karratha and join the north-west highway heading to Roebourne. Driving through the town, you'll see the police station on your right and the old gaol and tourist centre directly behind it. Plenty of history and an insight into the harsh conditions of yesteryear. You'll then need to do a U turn and travel back to the turn-off to Point Samson. On your way, you'll see a turn-off on your right to the historic town of Cossack, the centre of pearling and industry in the late 1800s. Wander the art gallery and the old court house museum. The short drive to Reader Head lookout provides 360 degree views over Settlers Beach. Point Samson is about 15 minutes away. It's a pleasant, quiet, laid-back sort of place. The beach at Honeymoon Cove is a popular haunt for the locals and worth a peek-a-boo if you're chasing a dip or a picnic.

The dilemma of
# ABORIGINAL ROCK ART

They reckon that by the end of this decade, the Egyptian pyramids will be closed down to protect them from tourists. Already, significant sites such as Stonehenge - once spray painted pink by vandals - have been cordoned off to the public. The Mona Lisa sits behind protective glass, its true colours hidden from the public eye forever, because some peanut ran amok and tried to slash it with a knife. Closer to home, in the Kimberley, dinosaur prints, preserved in stone for more than 400,000 years, were carved out of the rock to be sold on the black market (the culprit has since been caught and, hopefully, is breaking rocks now rather than stealing them).

So what does all this have to do with the Pilbara, I hear you ask. Well, regrettably, it could well be the sign of things to come, particularly in regard to the Aboriginal rock engravings in the region which, at least as far as tourists are concerned, remain largely undiscovered while authorities work out what to do to protect them. It's a challenge worth considering, particularly if you've arrived

in the Pilbara in search of a prominent site. According to the Western Australian Museum, the Pilbara is one of the richest Aboriginal rock engraving sites in the world and yet there is a reluctance to show tourists where the best sites are for fear they will get vandalised. And it only takes one idiot with another piece of rock, chiselling out some misguided testament of his love, to irreversibly deface a significant piece of art that's been sitting out there for 40,000 years. And when I say out there, we're talking hundreds of kilometres before you'll find anything that vaguely resembles a security guard! Of course the majority of people would respect the sites, see them as part of an ancient art gallery, revere them as time-capsules of a distant past. But you only have to visit Boodarrie Landing outside Port Hedland to see what can be done. Engravings of animals, spirit figures and various symbols have been vandalised. In one case, initials have been pneumatically chiselled into the rock, defacing what was obviously once a popular meeting place for Aboriginal people.

So what do you do? How do authorities provide access, yet ensure protection? Should tour operators be the only ones allowed to take tourists onto the sites? Should the sites be surrounded by fencing, and protective platforms be erected, as has been the case next to the BHP processing plant in Port Hedland. Is more education the answer? Should huge trespassing fines be imposed or should - as has been the case to date - discovery be left largely to chance, lengthy investigation or local knowledge. As you're on holiday, you might like to think about it: What would you do if you were the custodian of 40,000 years of Aboriginal art in the Pilbara?

**Note:** As you may have noticed, the locations of the carvings I have photographed have not been provided (Who am I, after all, to deny you the same satisfaction I have had in discovering them for myself?).

North-West Shelf
Gas Project

# THE NORTH-WEST SHELF GAS PROJECT

Imagine the logistics involved in having to right the main structure of a 54,000 tonne gas well in 120m of water to ensure it settled within centimetres of a small hole in the ocean bed. Consider what was needed to secure the massive North Rankin A Platform in "Cyclone Alley" and the engineering feat involved in linking it to the mainland with 135 km of underwater pipe, then processing and pumping the gas more than 1,500 km overland.

The North-West Shelf Gas Project is a monument to man's ingenuity -- a project of world-class significance which saw us reaching into the depths of the ocean and the earth to harness an alternative energy that today powers nations. It's Australia's single biggest engineering feat - bigger than the Snowy Mountains River Scheme - and, at $12 billion (back in the 1980s), it's also the nation's largest single commercial undertaking.

**Right:** The sinking of the huge well structure. **Far Right:** The North Rankin A Platform - a monument to man's ingenuity.

Sounds impressive huh? Well, it is, but to really appreciate the scale and importance of the project, you need to drop in to the Woodside Visitors' Centre at Dampier which overlooks the massive on-shore processing plant and gas storage and transfer facilities. The actual site looks like something out of a sci-fi movie -- huge green storage domes nestled like alien pods among mounds of rock; a city of pipes and chrome structures; towering gas flares which intermittently roar their defiance over the characteristic red boulder-strewn landscape of the Burrup Peninsula (...Someone shoot me with a laser, I'm having a prose attack!)

Anyway, while I'll leave it to the Visitors' Centre to impress you with facts, photos, figures, models and videos, here are some introductory snippets:

- That to find the gas the joint venturers spent 10 years surveying more than 80,000sq km of land -- more than half of which was under 180m of water, a third of which was under 460m of water - before they even put a well down.

-That the venture was a huge gamble, with 12 wells drilled over four years before commercial quantities of gas were actually discovered.

- That, at the time, no-where else in the world had gas been extracted from such depths.

**Above:** Woodside's gas refinement and processing plant at Dampier.

- That the main structure of the 54,000 tonne North Rankin A Platform - the first of the wells to be built - was towed from Japan (avoiding the typhoon season in the north and the cyclone season in the south).

- That the Rankin A Platform is held in place by 32 massive steel pipes driven 120m into the seabed.

- That the natural gas is condensed and liquified to occupy one six hundredth of the space of its gaseous form before being stored and transported by specially designed ships to Japan (you'll recognise the ships by their distinctive humps).

- That within four years of the completion of the North-West Shelf Natural Gas Project venture, natural gas was meeting more than half of Western Australia's non transport energy requirements.

- That more than 300,000 million cubic metres of natural gas are expected to be extracted from Rankin and Goodwin fields.

- That the North Rankin A Platform is one of the largest production gas capacity platforms in the world, capable of producing 46.7 million cubic metres of gas a day.

- That 34 wells are planned.

-That the North Rankin A Platform accommodates 118 permanent staff and 96 temporary staff, most of whom are flown in on two weeks on, one week off shifts.

All interesting stuff but, as I said, hard to appreciate without at least stopping in at the Visitors' Centre just half an hour out of Karratha.

For opening times contact the Karratha Tourist Bureau or the Visitors' Centre directly.

**Recommended Reading:** Beyond the Flame.

## Some Dates

1963-6: Woodside forms joint venture.

1971: Substantial reserves of natural gas discovered in North-West shelf.

1980: State government signs 20 year contract to receive gas supplies.

1981: Eight major Japanese companies sign up for gas supply.

1982: North Rankin A Platform "Splashdown".

1989: First LNG shipment arrives in Japan.

# *The* Montebell

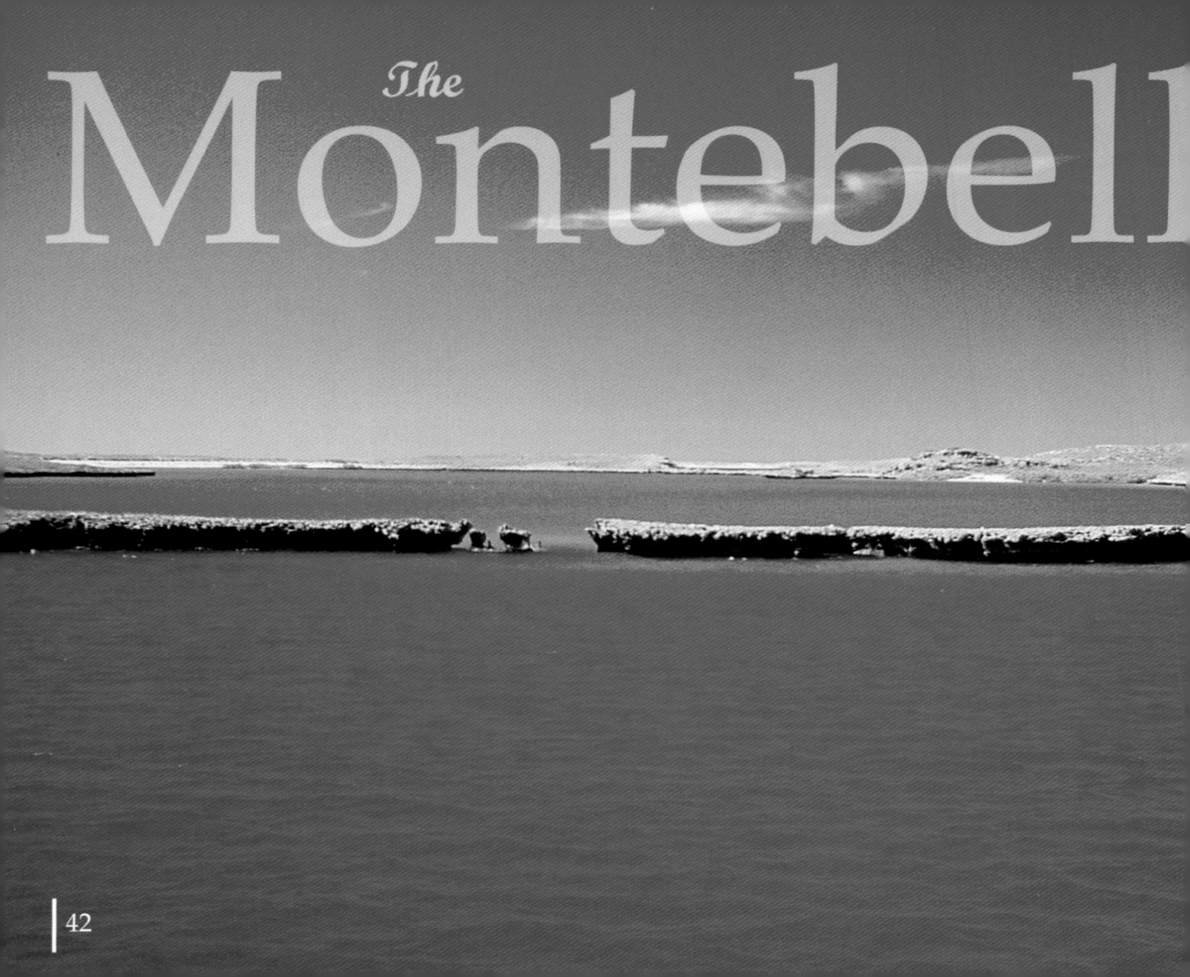

OS

Three pods of whales, dolphins, scores of turtles, prolific marine life to ponder through a dive mask and (are you ready for this?) a 28 kg Spanish Mackerel -- all during a three-day trip to the Montebello Islands off the Pilbara Coast.

I should confess that I'm not a fisherman (or fisherperson if you've got the sensitivities of a sea anemone). In fact, to be honest, I was handed the rod by someone who had been pulling them in all afternoon and needed to go to the toilet (A dedicated fisherman, he was the sort of guy who lunged for the gaff every time someone called "Whale"). Still, I enjoy the locations people like to fish from, so out to the Montebello Islands we headed.

We took a three day tour on a charter boat operating out of Dampier, heading through the Dampier Archipelago before making the five hour journey to reach what the locals affectionately call "The Montes". The conditions (in August) were excellent which

**Left:** The Montebello Islands, once a site for nuclear detonations.

43

made for a pleasant crossing (serious deliberation would be required in bad conditions).

The Montebello Islands are about 130km west of Dampier. About 100 limestone islands surrounded by white sandy beaches and turquoise green waters, the group has a 6m tidal range, which makes it great for snorkelling, beachcombing and exploring. Anchor between the islands and you'll find waters completely protected from the wind; stick your head underwater on neap tide and it's like looking into a glass aquarium.

The Montebello Islands have a bit of an ominous history. Back in 1952 the Poms needed a distant colonial outpost to detonate an atomic bomb and liked the Montebellos so much they exploded three before handing the islands back to the Australian Government in 1992 ( "She's all yours guvna, sorry 'bout the glow"). The experts say no harmful radiation exists though I was far from the last person to return to the boat after a wander on Trimouille Island where one of the bombs was detonated.

The islands also boast Western Australia's first shipwreck and a nautical yarn of high sea betrayal and intrigue. In 1622, using only a compass and a sounding lead to navigate, the 300 ton Tryal ran aground and slowly sank just off the Montebellos. Concerned the crew wouldn't see eye to eye with the Navy's policy of "captain and officers first; bugger the rest", Captain Brooke and a few of the lads snuck out the stern window to a waiting boat and a chest of gold, leaving the crew to swim for it. But, unbeknown to the captain, several crew made it to another boat and survived the 44 day, 2,000km journey back to Java, arriving within a week of the captain, who was billing himself as the local hero. Suffice to say, a few words were exchanged.

But back to the present day Montes. We snorkelled, fished and wandered all day, ate, sang and joked all night and, on day three, returned satisfied we'd visited one of the most remote islands off the Western Australian coast. Not a bad way to spend three days methinks. For more information about the Montebello Islands, contact the Karratha Tourist Bureau.

# Historic
# COSSACK

*A* visit to Cossack is a step into the past. After a walk through the courthouse museum and a few of the old government buildings, it's not difficult to imagine what it must have been like back in the 1880s when the town was the first port in the north-west -- a hustling, bustling frontier community; the centre of trade for the burgeoning pearling, gold and pastoral industries.

If you've done some background reading (*Cossack Gold* by W. Lambden Owen or Brian Hoey's *Cosssack, Land of the Silver Sea* are a good start) the old buildings which have been lovingly restored by successive caretakers whisper to you of a bygone era. Of a time when a cosmopolitan population of more than 400 people lived in the town, of the excited chatter of Asian divers from more than 80 vessels which combed nearby pearling fields, of gritty old prospectors hell bent on finding their fortunes. Many archaeological sites have been declared around Cossack as testament to its significance and, as you'll see from the museum collection, much has been uncovered to reveal the lifestyle of the town's early inhabitants. But while Cossack grew for more than 40 years, its decline was rapid (I reckon the sandflies may have had

**Right:** Cossack today.

something to do with it myself). When the pearling moved on to Broome and the goldrush rushed elsewhere, so did the population, and by the 1950s Cossack had become a ghost town. But unlike the original timber buildings which were secured to the ground in anticipation of cyclones by chains across the roof and huge boulders, the solid stone government buildings which followed still remain, some of which are today used as an art gallery, a cafe/restaurant and a backpacker hostel. If you want to just get away from it all and sit in silence appreciating what it must have been like when the north-west was first settled, this is the place to do it. ...Oh, and the locals reckon the fishing's not bad either.

# Karratha to Port Hedland

You're looking at about a two hour trip, assuming you're sticking to the speed limit and you don't want to stop off and have a look around (which sort of defies the reason you're on holiday, doesn't it?) If you're not in a hurry, I'd plan for at least a day trip, spending the morning doing a history lesson at Cossack before heading to Point Samson for lunch where the locals say they'd walk a hundred miles for the best fish and chips in the Pilbara. The turnoff's on your left, just before Roebourne. A 15 minute drive will see you in Cossack, another 15 and you're in Point Samson. As there's no ring road, you're looking at coming back the way you went in so if you're not sure, the best bet is to ask at the Karratha Tourist Bureau before you leave or go the couple of kilometres past the turnoff into Roebourne and ask a few questions at the old gaol. The gaol has been converted into the Roebourne Tourist Bureau. Plenty of helpful advice and good stuff to read and see while you're there (if for no other reason, drop in to see the conditions the prisoners were living in back in the "bad old days": Skin searing chains, 47 degree heat and the odd hanging). After Roebourne don't expect much until the Whim Creek Pub which is a great place for a break. It's the oldest Pub in the Pilbara, plenty of good yarns and cold drinks to be had. If you want an entertaining challenge, try getting that @###@!!! ring on the hook. After that, it's about an hour on to Port Hedland with not much in between. For the fishermen, Cleaverville and Balla Balla are popular haunts.

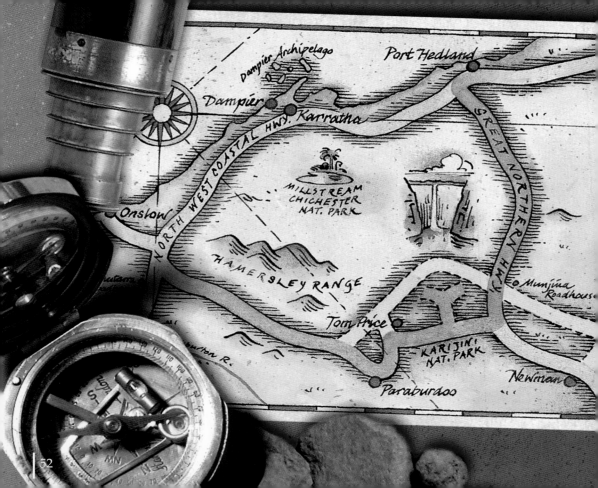

Dampier Archipelago

Port Hedland

Dampier

Karratha

GREAT NORTH WEST COASTAL HWY.

MILLSTREAM CHICHESTER NAT. PARK

Onslow

HAMERSLEY RANGE

GREAT NORTHERN HWY.

Munjina Roadhouse

Tom Price

KARIJINI NAT. PARK

Newman

Paraburdoo

52

# SUGGESTED ITINERARY
## Karijini Explorer - three days

**Nanutarra Roadhouse turnoff -- Tom Price - Karijini - Great Northern Highway (allow three days)**

Take a right-hand turn just after the Nanutarra Roadhouse to Tom Price where you can visit the Hamersley Iron Ore Mine and marvel at the huge earth moving equipment. Then stock up and head to Karijini National Park for some of the Pilbara's most spectacular scenery -- waterfalls, gorges, waterholes and spectacular tunnels of banded iron rock. Take one of the adventure trails, swim in one of the gorges or just take a leisurely stroll through a stunning landscape which has been more than 2 billion years in the making. Then head east until you reach the Great Northern Highway before heading north.

**Highlights:** Huge iron ore mine, gorges, waterholes and waterfalls of Karijini National Park.

# SOME TIPS FOR GOING OFF-ROAD

## LOW RANGE

Always remember: Low range is for getting you out of trouble, not into it!

## BOGGED IN SAND

Rarely will you remain bogged in sand if you let your tyres down to 15psi. Carry a pressure gauge and a portable compressor if you plan a lot of sand work.

## WATER CROSSING

If you're unsure about the crossing ahead of you, get out of the car and walk it first. When crossing a deep river, place a tarp between your engine and your bumper bar and keep the bow wave just ahead of you. Try and cross in one smooth motion. Don't change gears ('cause you'll get water in the clutch).

## TRAVELLING IN CONVOY

When travelling in convoy, remember your responsibility is to the person behind you.

## WATER AND FUEL

Always carry a spare jerry can of water and fuel.

## TOWING

When towing, make sure the connections on to which you're attaching the tow line are attached to the car's chassis. Horror stories abound of bull bars and tow bars being torn off and taking with them limbs and body pieces.

## STOP AND THINK

If you find yourself in trouble stop and take the time to properly consider your options. Ten minutes in thought could save you several hours of inconvenience.

## AUTHOR'S TOP TIP

If, like me, you're lost when it comes to all things mechanical, rent a satellite telephone. That way you're never alone.

# 4X4 ADV<sup>E</sup>NTURE

It's a sad reflection of the company I keep that four people who have travelled with me in the same car sponsored me to do a four wheel drive course. (they say a near death experience can do that to you!). Having completed the course, however, I would highly recommend it, not only as a safe way to learn about driving in demanding conditions but also as a great way to explore parts of the Pilbara that most visitors rarely get to see. Four wheel driving courses are organised through the colleges in the Pilbara and, in Port Hedland and Karratha, there is a company called Opposite Lock (which, coincidentally, sells four wheel drive accessories) that offers "tag along" weekends for small groups. They organise the trips through private properties and you just turn up with your car, pay a charge to cover costs and you're away. To the experts it may all seem like rudimentary stuff but, as the course I went on demonstrated, a lot is assumed about the owners of four wheel drive vehicles. Over three days we did river crossings, steep climbs, vehicle recoveries and basic maintenance. I learned how to effortlessly extract myself from bogs, throw my car headlong into a river and scale obstacles I would previously have gone around. Understanding my vehicle's capabilities was one of the greatest benefits, while having the support of people who knew what they were doing gives you the confidence to experiment a bit. As to the four who sponsored me, they should take some comfort knowing that at least now if I leave the road at 160 km/h, I have a fair idea of how to get back on!

**Left:** Kids, don't try this at home. The four wheel drive course found me another medium to run amok in: water!

# Karratha to Millstream

There are two ways into Millstream from the coast -- the Hamersley access road from Karratha (which follows Hamersley's rail line to Tom Price) or the Millstream road off the North-west Coastal Highway about 40 km north of Karratha. If I were travelling north and wanted to see **The Millstream Chichester National Park,** I'd pull in for a night at Karratha to shower and stock up, organise a permit to travel on the access road (available free through the Karratha Tourist Bureau) and plan a circuit that saw me camping out for a couple of nights and coming back through Pyramid station and out onto the Great Northern Highway to head further north. Expect to spend three hours getting to Millstream along the unsealed road and about the same to get back onto the highway (which allows for a swim at **Python Pool**). Highlights of the journey include the meandering drive up on to the Chichester Range, the spectacular views from **Panorama Lookout** , a swim or camp at Python Pool, a wander along the old cameleers trail at **Mt Herbert,** the plateau of sweeping spinifex plains, and the mountains of iron encrusted rubble. After a rain (February), it's particularly pleasant. The spinifex is green and a metre high. For a memorable moment (refer picture following page) try and catch the dramatic cloud formations from Panorama Lookout as the storms roll in from the coast (though be prepared to camp if the rain that follows is heavy).

**Right:** Python Pool

**Python Pool:** It sounds like the sort of place Indiana Jones would hang out, however, Python Pool has nothing to do with its namesake (and believe me, if it had, I'd be the last one to have swum there!). Where its name came from, no one seems to know.

A perennial waterhole, Python Pool lies at the western base of the Chichester Ranges. It's a large rock pool surrounded by overhanging gum trees and smooth boulders, with a towering sheer rock backdrop and a crack in the wall that promises a spectacular waterfall if you were there during a deluge. Apart from being a pleasant place for a swim, Python Pool is historically significant as it was well used by the cameleers who pioneered the western interior and carried much-needed supplies to inland settlements from Cossack in the late 1800s. In fact, the old supply road which leads up the range is a short walk from the pool. Just head left along the range until you come to the base of the meandering paved trail and an old stone reinforcement.

# The Old Camel Trail (8 km walk)

If you're feeling energetic and you're into bushwalking and scenery, the best way to appreciate the old Camel Trail is to walk the 8km from the Mt Herbert car park (about 15 minutes drive further up the road) back to Python Pool. You'll need two cars unless you want to do the return journey. The road's historical significance as the main supply artery between the north-west port at Cossack and inland stations

**Above:** A flock of Emus make their way across the Pilbara plains. **Right:** Rainclouds gather in the distance from Mt Herbert Lookout.

such as Millstream and Tambrey saw 8 km of it made into a walk trail as part of a bicentennial project. Small yellow triangles with camels on them mark the trail for easy orientation. On a mild day it's a pleasant walk (as in no huffing and puffing) which will see you wandering for two or three hours through rolling spinifex plains and iron encrusted hills. You pass McKenzies Pool which has water all year round and a few Aboriginal rock engravings (though you might need a trained eye to see them). Obviously a lot of work was involved in building the road, particularly when you appreciate most of it was done by hand. Much of it is cobblestoned and "catch-alls" have been cut in to the trail to deflect water. Intricate rock walls have been built to reinforce the road and you can see where gunpowder has been used to persuade stubborn boulders to step aside.

In all, walking the trail is not a bad way to work up a bit of a sweat and, if the panoramic view over the Roebourne Plains from the top of the range isn't reward enough, the plunge into Python Pool at the end of the walk certainly should be.

**Above:** Walking the old Camel Trail. **Right:** Reflections at Millstream.

Millstream

According to Aboriginal mythology, Millstream was created in the Dreaming by the Rainbow Serpent "Warlu", which burrowed into the landscape to create many of the natural features of the Pilbara. Having made the Fortescue River and an oasis at Millstream earlier, the serpent was travelling from the coast when it rose from the ground to the smell of birds being cooked. According to ancient law it was prohibited to catch and cook those particular birds. Enraged, Warlu dived back into the ground and surfaced at Millstream to find two young boys eating the birds. In anger, the Dreamtime serpent flooded the area and drowned the two boys as an example to anyone else who broke the ancient law.

Today the Aborigines of the Pilbara revere Millstream as one of the region's most significant sites. As a sign of respect for Warlu and the land, some Aborigines still arrive at the banks of the river or streams and fill their mouths with water then blow it back into the river calling out the name of the serpent.

**Left:** Looking out across the Fortescue River, near Millstream Homestead.

# INVASION OF THE DATE PALMS

Millstream Homestead is surrounded by picturesque settings -- rivers banked by eucalyptus trees and waterholes shaded by lush palms. The abundance of water it enjoys year round has made it the home for a wide variety of rare insects, particularly dragonflies, damselflies and the odd (surely I jest) fruit bat. While most visitors would see a tranquil, oasis setting just behind the old homestead, the site has become a war zone over recent years as CALM (The Department for Conservation and Land Management) seeks to wreste back the land from the predatory date palms which were introduced by settlers late in the 19th century. The Millstream Palms which are seen only in five other areas of the Pilbara fell victim to the date palms' predatory nature, their towering fronds preventing the plants from receiving light, their fibrous root systems stealing their water. Adding to the problem was the abundance of dead fronds from the date palms which have proved to be a major fire hazard. In recent years CALM has begun a management program to liberate the river pools and springs from the Date Palms. It's an interesting study in environmental management and, well, if you have to study, you couldn't ask for a better classroom.

**Above:** Oasis setting near Millstream Homestead. **Right:** Camping in the Pilbara

**Picture:** Mount Bruce

# Karijini
### National Park

*Y*ou're sitting on the wooden platform sharing Fern Pool with a group of foreign tourists, when one woman, down by the water, completes her cigarette and drops it into the pool, then walks away. Would you pretend you didn't see it and look the other way? Tell someone else, hoping they'll do something about it? Pick it up yourself? Or tap the lady on the shoulder, tell her it's a sensitive environment and suggest she fishes it out?

**Previous Page and above:** Fern Pool, one of the many spectacular, and extremely sensitive, sites of Karijini National Park. **Right:** Weano Gorge.

## Grading Guide

✱
Good scenery. My Mum could do it.

✱ ✱
Relatively easy, a bit of risk if you want it.

✱ ✱ ✱
Some huffing and puffing involved. You need to be reasonably fit to enjoy it.

✱ ✱ ✱ ✱
Demanding, a bit dangerous

✱ ✱ ✱ ✱ ✱
Indiana Jones material Dangerous and demanding. A top adventure if you're fit!

# Warning

There have been people killed at Karijini National Park so it goes without saying the walks can be dangerous. There's the height thing (a100m fall tends to take it out of you a bit), the cold water (temperatures can plunge to near freezing), exhaustion (hiking out can be a killer) and getting lost before dying from hypothermia ("I'm sure the turnoff is here somewhere"). But all of this can be avoided with a bit of common sense and planning. For a start, if you're planning one of the adventure trails, make sure your first stop is the ranger's station where you can gather detailed information about the walks that interest you. A quick phone call and you might be able to tag on to a tour with one of the local operators who specialise in the adventure trails. Apart from that, it's a matter of being sensible - knowing your limits, not going beyond where you are confident of getting back, taking appropriate food and water and letting others know when you're setting off.

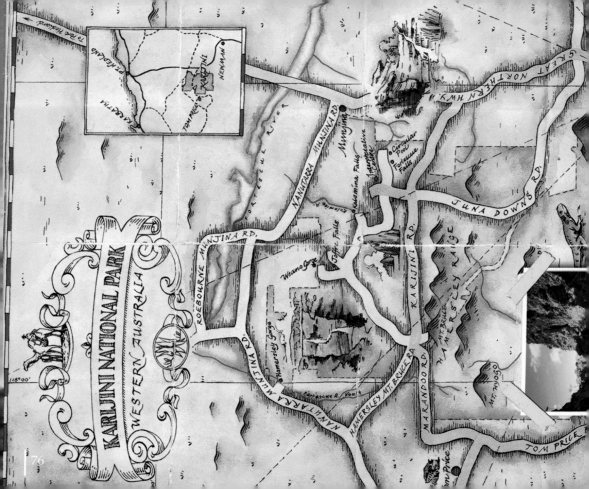

KARIJINI NATIONAL PARK

WESTERN AUSTRALIA

118°00'

TO Port Hedland

PIT HEDLAND

KARIJINI

TOM PRICE

NEWMAN

GREAT NORTHERN HWY

FORTESCUE RIVER

NANUTARRA MUNJINA RD.

MUNJINA RD.

Munjina

Circular Pool

Fortescue Falls

Interpretative Centre

Kalamina Falls

JUNA DOWNS RD.

ROEBOURNE MUNJINA RD.

Joffre Falls

Weano Gorge

KARIJINI RD.

HAMERSLEY RANGE

NANUTARRA MUNJINA RD.

Hamersley Gorge

Fortescue R. South

HAMERSLEY MT. BRUCE RD.

MARANDOO RD.

MT. BRUCE

MT. MOGO

Tom Price

TOM PRICE

76

# Karijini Walk Trails

While one of the big attractions of Karijini National Park is that its scenery is so accessible - you can literally pull into a car park, walk 50m and peer into a 100m canyon to see waterfalls and emerald coloured rock pools -.to me the great appeal of Karijini lies deep within its gorges. The Karijini experience is all about adventure. It's about exploring the serpentine tunnels of marbled rock, clambering over boulders and squeezing through narrow tunnels, inching your way along ledges, paddling or wading through subterranean waterways and descending deep into chasms which have been eroded into the landscape over two billion years. It's about the thrill of having done one of the harder walks, sharing the experience and going to where few have been.

But, truth be told, most of us are unlikely to commit serious energy to a walk (particularly a gorge walk) if we are not assured that what we see at the bottom will be worth the effort. So I've put together a brief overview of some of the main walks of the park. As you will see, each walk has its own distinct character and, in my opinion, all of them are worth the effort. But if you're limited by time and energy, the following pages should help you decide which ones you want to do.

Karijini Visitor Centre

# Dales Gorge

**Above:** Fortesque Falls. **Right and following page:** Ferns Pool.

Fortescue Falls and Fern Pool would have to be the two highlights of Dales Gorge. The descent to the falls is relatively easy and safe (you can see it from the top). At a leisurely pace, it should take you about 15 minutes. At the bottom of the trail you can head right to Fern Pool or left for the three hour walk to Circular Pool. **Fern Pool** is about 10 minutes away and would have to be one of the most picturesque settings in the park. It has water all year round, with two 10m waterfalls cascading into a large swimming hole that's surrounded by huge fig and paperbark trees. The moist rock ledges by the falls are dripping with ferns. You don't have to be David Suzuki to see this is a particularly sensitive area so stick to the platform and be careful not to damage the

# Dales at a glance

**TIME:** Allow two hours for Fortescue Falls and Fern Pool, three hours for the walk around to Circular Pool.

**BEST TIME OF YEAR:** All year round.

**GRADE:**
Fortescue Falls and
Fern Pool ✳✳✳
Circular Pool ✳✳✳

**HIGHLIGHT:** Fantastic swimming hole and waterfalls.

**NEED TO TAKE:** Snack and an air mattress for Fern Pool if you're feeling decadent)

**START:** Fortescue Falls Carpark.

**FINISH:** As above.

foliage. If you've got children, this is a good place to teach them about respect for the environment. After a bit of a swim, the more energetic can wander back to Fortescue Falls and down along Dales Gorge to Circular Pool (allow three hours). The walk is pleasant and typical of what you'll experience in the wide basins of the Karijini gorges. The patterns and colours of the ancient rock - rich ochres, reds and blues - are a constant source of interest. The swim at Circular Pool will hopefully, provide the rejuvenation you'll need prior to the steep climb up the gorge wall.

**Helpful Hints:** Fortescue Falls or Fern Pool is a great place for a picnic. If you want to "do" Circular Pool without the three hour walk, there is a track leading from the lookout directly above it. Fern Pool - once called Hidden Pool by the locals - is likely to become increasingly popular, so get there early if you want it to yourself.

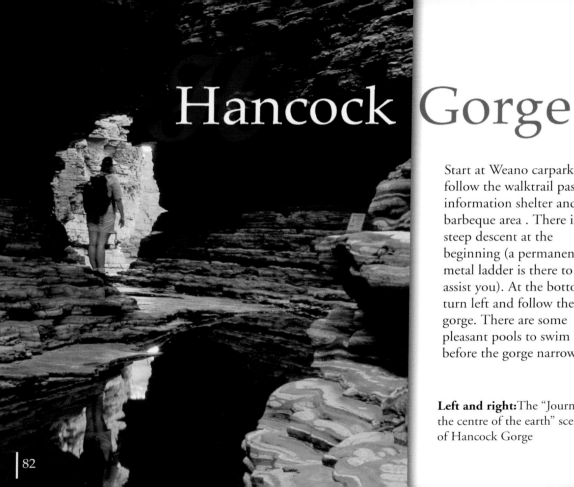

# Hancock Gorge

Start at Weano carpark a
follow the walktrail past
information shelter and
barbeque area . There is
steep descent at the
beginning (a permanent
metal ladder is there to
assist you). At the bottor
turn left and follow the
gorge. There are some
pleasant pools to swim ir
before the gorge narrows

**Left and right:**The "Journe
the centre of the earth" scen
of Hancock Gorge

and descends into a huge chamber and what I think is one of the most attractive settings in Karijini. At the bottom of the stream which flows through a corridor of marbled rock is a swimming hole which turns a deep emerald green when the sunlight shines on it. The glowing walls of the winding gorge beyond provide a stunning backdrop. From there, the second leg of the walk starts which, as you can see, is steep and, unless you're with an experienced guide or someone who knows their way around, I wouldn't recommend it. There are some dangerous ledges to get around. One which left a lasting impression on me involved crawling around a 90 degree corner on my knees above a 10m drop while clinging for dear life to a small piece of wire thoughtfully embedded in the rock. There's a bit of swimming to do, a treacherous climb down a steep, slippery wall, a vertical ascent up a rock chimney and edging your way along a 20m cliff face. Having survived it, however, I'd highly recommend the adventure. But don't try it without a guide as you'll probably still be wandering the gorges days later because you've missed the turn to get out! There's a good reason why

# Hancock at a glance

**TIME:** Allow 6 hours

**BEST TIME OF YEAR:** February - May, September -November

**GRADE:** *****

**HIGHLIGHT:** Journey to the Centre of the Earth scenery.

**NEED TO TAKE:** Garbage bag to keep things dry

**START:** Weano Information Shelter

**FINISH:** As above

the journey is called The Miracle Mile. It's because, by the end of it, you'll think it's a bloody miracle you survived!

**Helpful hints:** Carry a garbage bag to keep things dry, take a cut lunch and a couple of energy bars, and - importantly - if you haven't planned to do the whole trip, don't go beyond the point where you are confident you could get back if you had to.

**Afternote:** Since I left, an abseiling tour has been set up. Now that would be the way to do it! There are also several tour operators who specialise in the gorges. Ask at any one of the tourist bureaus for more information.

*There's a good reason it's called "The Miracle Mile". It's because by the end of it, you'll think it's a bloody miracle you survived!*

# Joffre Falls

**Above :** Joffre Falls.
**Right:** Joffre Gorge (don't forget to take an inner tube if you're planning the walk/float)

The Joffre Gorge walk starts at the Joffre Falls carpark. Then head left, as you need to cross the top of the falls before descending into the gorge. The first part is fun (chucking your tyre tube down ahead of you makes climbing easier) and the initial paddle and short walk at the bottom are a good taste of what's ahead. The Aborigines used to camp on top of Joffre Falls where food was plentiful. (it still is, if you know where to look). The first challenge is a 5m drop/jump into a large pool (you can pass down your camera gear). After that, it's fairly smooth paddling and walking. The scenery is picturesque and varies. You can

# Joffre at a glance

**TIME:** Allow six hours (or an hour around the waterfall)

**BEST TIME OF YEAR:** February - May, September -November.

**GRADE:** ∗∗∗

**HIGHLIGHTS:** Leisurely paddling through the narrow gorges with 30m walls on either side.

**NEED TO TAKE:** Inner Tube.

**START:** Joffre Falls

**FINISH:** Knox Gorge carpark

**ADVICE:** See Ranger for Trail Guide.

be paddling- mouth agape and eyes to the heavens - along narrow waterways flanked by 100 metre high walls or you can be walking through expansive basins with overhanging trees and crystal clear pools. It's a long trek and save a bit of energy for the last leg of the journey. At the exit several hundred metres before the junction of Red and Hancock gorges, things get a bit tough. You're looking at a 60 degree ascent up the gorge wall and a vertical climb near the top. Then you have the kilometre walk across the spinifex to Knox carpark. All up though, it's well worth it. Rest assured, you'll sleep well that night!

**Helpful hints:** See the ranger for a Trail Guide (or you won't know where to get out), wear a pair of shoes you're prepared to drown for the sake of a good adventure, carry a couple of extra energy bars, put the stuff you need to stay dry inside a garbage bag in your pack, let down your tube for the final ascent and - importantly - pick a time of year when it's not too hot and the water isn't too cold (or you'll freeze your butt off!). Best months: March/April. Oh, and one last thing: If yours is the car left at Knox Carpark to take everyone back to the car at Joffre's, make sure you don't leave your keys in their car (it cost me a @@@###!!! carton of beer!).

**Right:** Handrail Pool, Weano Gorge. Story next page.

# Weano Gorge

To me, Weano Gorge and Handrail Pool is the best introduction to the walks of Karijini. It has a little bit of everything and it's not too difficult (though it can be incredibly slippery if there is water running). You have a relatively easy walk down steps to the basin. Turn right for a short meander between the layered rock walls and paperbark pools then climb down into the narrow marbled crevice which leads to Handrail Pool. The reason it's called Handrail becomes apparent, as that ( and a piece of rope) is what you'll be holding on to to get down to the water. The pool itself is quite large, surrounded by 20m rock walls except for a crevice that leads further back. If you're feeling intrepid and would like a bit of a climb (plan for about an hour there and back), paddle the pool, scuttle across the rocks and head into the crevice. The climbing is quite easy as the smooth layered rock provides good footing and something to hold on to. At times, the thin ledges and height can be a bit daunting but the secret is to take your time and make sure at least two parts of your body (ie a hand and a foot - are securely placed at any one time).

Wandering about waist-high through the water before climbing back on the ledge, you soon come to a steep drop-off and a long pool. If you walk to the edge, you can step down quite easily to another ledge and walk around. This, to me, is what the gorges of Karijini are all about; shafts of light flooding the chamber, the warm orange glow of the rock walls beyond, the sound of cascading water, smooth marbled surfaces and the pristine, emerald green pools. It's been going on for hundreds of thousands of years so take a few minutes to take it in. If you continue along the ledge, you need to descend to the basin where you can swim back into the pool or climb down further into a large, open area and a setting similar to Handrail. Beyond that a short walk takes you to the edge of a major precipice, from where you can see the base of Red Gorge well below. Unless you're planning a short life, this is where to turn back. **Helpful hints:** From Handrail Pool, you can do most of the walk in bare feet (or diving booties work for me). Take along a snack. Make sure the water's not too cold. If you want to sunbake, best to get there around midday when the sun's shining directly into the gorge.

# Weano at a glance

**TIME:** Allow one hour for Handrail, two hours to explore beyond.

**BEST TIME OF YEAR**: All year round (if you can handle cold water!).

**GRADE:** ✶✶

**HIGHLIGHT:** Swimming holes, scenery, narrow chasms, plenty of variety.

**NEED TO TAKE:** Snack

**START:** Information Shelter at Weano carpark.

**FINISH:** As above.

Now this is the way to see the gorges -- comfortably seated at five thousand feet! If you haven't been in a helicopter before - particularly a three seater with the doors taken off - flying over Karijini is a great way to be initiated. Don the headset, clip on the seatbelt, sit around while the pilot does his pre-flight check and ... lift off. The whirring rotors, the tilt, the surge forward, the rushing air and then, suddenly, the stunning Karijini landscape unfolds beneath you. Quite simply, it's a magic experience, particularly flying over the park on a warm evening as the setting sun paints the sky a deep mauve and inflames the tops of the Hamersley Range. While the light early or late in the day creates an unforgettable mood, a flight in broad daylight offers a brighter bird's eye view of one of the oldest landscapes in the world. If you've put in the effort to wander the gorges beforehand, there's something particularly satisfying about effortlessly traversing the land from the air. In less than a minute you have crossed a steep ravine or circled a mountain bluff. You can be peering deep into a 100m gorge from directly above, hovering over a waterfall, or looking out into the distant horizon across the sculptured landscape of mountains and hills which were once the seabed of a primordial ocean -- 360 degree views as far as the eye can see. Truth be told, no photograph can do it justice. To appreciate it, you simply need to be there. Catch it when the light is right, and the experience is likely to be the highlight (literally) of your holiday.

**Note:** At the time of publication, it seemed uncertain whether helicopter flights were going to be continued over the park. If it does cease, probably the best way to get it going again is to register your interest with the Pilbara's tourist bureaus, so the next time a local aerial cattle musterer considers supplementing his income by flying the odd tourist about, he'll/she'll know there's plenty of interest. It might not get you in the air this visit but, hopefully, you will get the chance to fly when you come back.

I guess you had to be there at the time. There I was at 5.00am in pitch darkness, with a photographer, a creative director and two models, making our way down the winding track towards the end of Oxer Lookout (right) so we'd be in position by sunrise to take this photograph. It was the final day of an intense week-long photo shoot. We had all arrived at the campsite nearby late the night before and, as I had done the reconnaissance a week earlier and was the only one who had been to Oxer Lookout before, I led the group down onto the precipice to where we'd set up for the picture. Simon, the photographer, was in good spirits, as were the two models, but Vaughan, the creative director,

had fallen behind and was having trouble with his contact lenses.

It was about when we reached the point at Oxer Lookout - as the sun started to come up and the yawning abyss appeared on either side of us - that a blood-curdling scream filled the gorges. A short way back Vaughan had fallen, but only to all fours, and was hugging a rock wall, suffering from the worst (yet most entertaining) case of vertigo I have ever witnessed. I suspect he regretted having ever secured his contact lenses as the view they afforded him had turned him sheet white and saw him sweating so much it looked like someone had turned on a hidden faucet. Clinging to the rock like a limpet, his babbling made no sense at all. It was some time before all four of us were able to wrench him away and get him back up to what he believed was safe ground. From there he eventually directed the photo shoot with his back to the scene, using Polaroid pictures which were passed up to him. Suffice to say, since then, I have trouble looking at this photo and thinking of anything else.

**Note: Since this picture was taken, the last 50m of Oxer Lookout has been closed to the public for safety reasons and two viewing platforms have been opened nearby.**

**Above:** Looking down into Junction Pool. **Right:** This is where the "Spider Act" starts.

# Knox Gorge

Start at Knox Carpark and head off down into the gorge. If you're doing the four-hour wander, head left at the bottom (to the right there's a pleasant, shaded swimming hole). The gorge basin is wide to start, though you have to walk along narrow ledges on either side if you want to avoid getting your feet wet. At the end of a large pool, the gorge becomes narrow and descends steeply -- which is where things get a bit tricky. After throwing your tyre inner tube ahead of you, you climb down and eventually have to turn sideways, pushing against your back with your feet and inching your way down. You're literally wedged between two rock walls in a seated position, about 2m above a thin torrent of water which disappears into the depths below. The prospect of losing your footing looms large in your mind. Drop, and you're likely to have a serious ankle injury (and if you do, God knows how you'll get out!). About halfway down, you have to suspend yourself with your arms and swivel your body to get around a corner. It's about now the old legs start to get a bit rubbery, but there's relief (if you can call it that) just around the corner -- a natural rock slide that ends in a 10m drop into a deep pool. Yahooooo! (If you've got camera gear, make sure it's wrapped in a garbage bag in your back pack and hold it above your head as you fall). Suffice to say, by this stage there is no going back (though, in my opinion, that point was passed the minute we started our spider act!). A short swim across to the other side, stand up and it's the same again, but from a bit higher up (make sure you jump well out into the middle to avoid the rocks).   Another big surge of adrenalin. Again, yahooooo! By now you're at the bottom of the gorge and a short swim through a crevice sees you back into the daylight and a large pool -- which is when the inner tube comes in handy. From there it's a leisurely paddle and walk to the left down Red Gorge until you reach Joffre and the final, demanding ascent back up to the top. Then you've got the walk across the spinifex back to the Carpark.

**Helpful hints:** The trek requires fitness and strength. If you can't handle a 10m jump into a pool, don't go. See the ranger for the Trail  Guide (or you won't know where to get out), let down your tube for the final ascent and pick a time of year when the water isn't too cold.

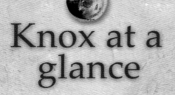

# Knox at a glance

**TIME:** Allow four hours

**BEST TIME OF YEAR:** February - May, September - November

**GRADE**: ✶✶✶✶

**HIGHLIGHT:** Two 10m, adrenalin pumping, jumps into a pool

**NEED TO TAKE:** Inner tube.

**START:** Knox Gorge carpark.

**FINISH:** Knox Gorge carpark

**ADVICE:** Do the trip with an experienced guide or, at the very least, see the ranger for information. If you haven't planned for the whole walk, don't go beyond the point where you're confident you could get back if you had to.

**Picture:** Karijini National Park

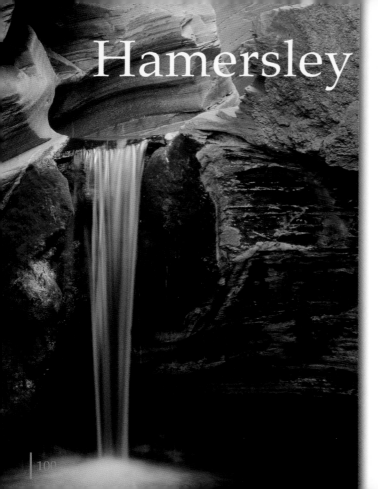

# Hamersley Gorge

Think pleasant waterhole paddle, climbing up gently sloping rock walls and bathing in your own private (well, that's assuming no one else is there!) natural spa and you're beginning to get a feel for what Hamersley Gorge has to offer. There's also the explore up or down the gorge following the flow of water and the spectacular wave of rock that forms the backdrop to the waterhole area (following page). The huge layered wave of rock stands as a lasting testament to the forces which tore away at the earth and caused the gorges of Karijini. It's a pleasant break in the drive if you're coming up around the park from Tom Price (or vice versa). Don't forget the picnic lunch.

Grade: *

**Left** and **right:** Hamersley Gorge

**Picture:** Karijini National Park

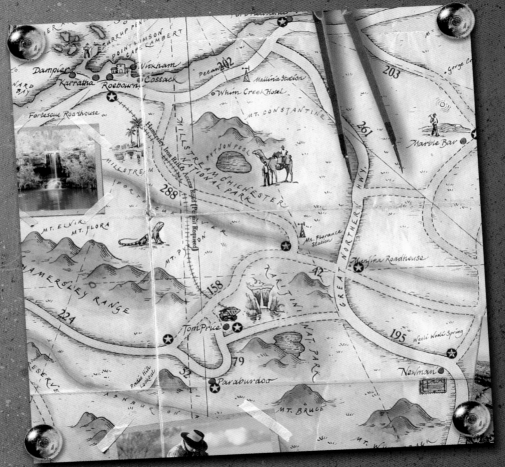

# Tom Price

A small working community built around Hamersley's massive iron ore mine, Tom Price rightly competes as the Gateway to Karijini National Park (it also vigorously pursues the state's Tidy Town awards which it's won on many occasions). The town has caravan, camping and hotel accommodation, which provides for that much needed shower and a respite from the heat and occasional subzero temperatures of the park, and you can pick up petrol and supplies. If you haven't done a mine tour before, this is the place (so's Newman for that matter). Massive trucks and other earthmoving equipment make for interesting viewing and, if you're lucky, you may catch one of those mighty explosions that dislodge huge chunks of the mountainside. Tours leave regularly from the Tourist Information Bureau, which is always worth the visit for a chat and local information.

**Left:** Panoramic view from Mt Nameless, 1,128m above sea level. **Right:** "Big" is what you'll see at the mine site.

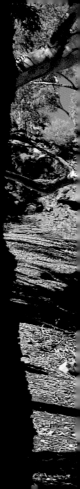

# Newman

Gateway to the Western Desert
and the northern goldfields

# Newman

Newman, like Tom Price, is a small working community built around BHP's massive Mt Whaleback iron ore mine. Like Tom Price, it offers mine tours, that much needed shower, cooked food and supplies. But - at least to me - while Tom Price is the gateway to Karijini, Newman is the gateway to the Western Desert, the northern goldfields and a chance to gain some insight into traditional Aboriginal culture. It is here you can head for the Canning Stock Route or out to Rudall River National Park. This is the last real "watering hole" if you're heading east. If you're heading north it's up through the goldfields, on to Nullagine and Marble Bar. There's a waterhole circuit if you feel like doing a short explore around Newman but, again, best to stop in at the Tourist Information Centre for helpful advice and local knowledge as your remote outback experience is likely to start from here.

**Previous Page:** Wanna Munna waterhole near Newman.
**Right:** One of the many giant trucks at the Newman mine

# First Contact

Many visitors to the Pilbara arrive with some expectation of coming into contact with traditional Aboriginal culture yet, in reality, most are likely to see only the occasional full-blood wandering through the supermarket on government payday or a group of Aboriginal people sitting beneath the shade of a nearby tree. Sadly, the most vivid impression many people leave the Pilbara with is of the displaced Aborigine who has turned to alcohol and loiters in public places.

In the Pilbara, the solution to how two vastly different cultures co- exist is no less complex than anywhere else in Australia and visitors seeking an insight into the issues might best start by reading about the history of white settlement in the region. But be warned, it's a sad chapter. Within most balanced accounts you'll read of how the white settlers arrived in the late 19th century and claimed the land as their own, bringing with them cattle, boundaries and laws that saw the Aborigine displaced and driven into the desert. There are sad accounts of how the Aboriginal population was decimated by the pestilence introduced by the white settlers, how they were indentured and used as slave labour, how they sought to flee harsh conditions only to be returned under the law in chains and how they were banished to starve to death at the whim of their employers.

From the moment early explorer William Dampier described Aborigines as the most miserable creatures on earth, their fate seemed sealed. Without their land and the traditional social systems that bound them to it, their rich, 40,000 year old culture went into rapid decline, so much so that by the 1930s the Aboriginal race faced extinction.

It is a sad chapter indeed but, as you will discover, one brought about largely by ignorance about the Aboriginal people and, over time, a tendency to judge them on a sorry appearance to which white Australia has largely contributed.

In this new era of reconciliation and hope, it is important to understand what brought the Aboriginal people to this point so we don't make the same mistakes of the past ...something maybe we should all bear in mind the next time we see a full-blood Aborigine wandering through the supermarket.

**Some fine background reading:** *The Nor Westers* by Jennie Hardy, *How the West was Lost* by Don McLeod, *Gold Dust and Iron Mountains* by Hugh Edwards, *The Pilbara - Cradle of an Ancient Civilisation* by Bill Quinn and (one of my favourites) *The Songlines* by Bruce Chatwin.

**Right:** Historic photographs are a grim testament to a harsh time in the West.

# SUGGESTED ITINERARY
## Pilbara Four Wheel Drive adventure
### (Two days)

**Newman - Nullagine - Marble Bar - North-West Coastal Highway**
(refer  map facing page)

From Newman follow the road signs pointing to Nullagine and Marble Bar. Take a journey along the graded road through the ancient Pilbara landscape to Nullagine. Journey through the pockmarked landscape of the surrounding goldfields and relive the heady goldrush days of the 1890's.
If you want to get further off the beaten track, take a couple of days to explore the goldfields circuit out along Skull Springs road. Camp out at one of the paperbark waterholes or wander the fringes of the Great Sandy Desert.

Many a bush verse has been written about the route between Nullagine and Marble Bar -- Australia's hottest town. Today most travellers like to just say they've had a beer at the Ironclad Hotel

**Highlights:**
Pristine waterholes, Nullagine Goldfields, Australia's hottest town, the old Comet Mine and the blood red jasper of Coppins Gap.

# JOURNEY ACROSS
# THE WESTERN INTERIOR

Heard of Colonel Peter Egerton Warburton?

Well, neither had I until I came to the Pilbara. Now, singlehandedly, he has shattered any romantic notion I ever had of wanting to return to a past life as an explorer. Colonel Warburton was the first person to traverse the western interior of Australia - or terra incognita, as it was known late in the 19th century -- and what a read his book makes. While the first half is taken up with background notes and an observation that the Colonel had little interest in writing his memoirs beyond the obligatory report to satisfy the sponsors of his expedition, the second half - his journal - is fascinating reading. We're talking serious hardship: travelling 4,000 miles on camels from Adelaide to Roebourne through the worst of what Australia had to offer; a journey on which they set off carrying six month's provisions which took two years to complete. It's an easy and gripping read as the Colonel was obviously not prone to long-winded log entries and deals with his circumstance matter-of-factly:

**On sleep:** *"Toiled along for 20 miles; hoped to have got an hour or two's sleep, but the ants forbade it. Night work, tropical heat, no sleep,* *poor food and a very limited allowance of water are, when combined, enough to reduce a man's strength; it is no wonder then that I can scarcely crawl. What a country. Did ever men before traverse such a tract of desert? I think not."*

**On ants:** *"Another 20 miles. Again tormented with ants, and could get no rest. They will not allow us to have any shade. I cannot stay under a bush but am compelled in sheer despair to throw myself on the burning sand, and let the sun pour down on me."*

**On food:** *"Richard shot me a little bird. It was only the size of a Sparrow but it did me good. If the country would only give any single thing we could eat, I should do well but we cannot find a snake, Kite or Crow...we are at our last drop of water and the smallest bit of dried meat chokes me."*

**On cooking camel feet:** *"Light a good fire some time beforehand, and let the wood burn down to bright glowing embers, cut the foot off at the hock and scrape and singe as much hair off it as time and appetite will permit. Having done this, stick the end into the glowing coals, burn it for some considerable time and*

**Right:** The Rudall River area.

*then, withdrawing it, place it on its side on the ground and strike the other side smartly with the back of a tomahawk, when if charred enough, the sole will come off a large flat slab composed of tough spongy horn; if it refuses to part with the flesh, stuff it into the fire again until it becomes more reasonable. This would seem rather a long process for a hungry man to perform and the reader further task but to devour the dainty morsel. Not so. Having got the sole off, place the foot in the bucket and keep it steadily boiling for 36 hours. If your fire goes out or you drop asleep, of course it will require longer. Then at last you may venture the hope that your teeth -- if good -- will enable you to masticate your long deferred dinner."*

**On death**: *"As for myself, I can see no hope of life, for I cannot hold up without food or water. I have given Lewis written instructions to justify his leaving me, should I die."*

All in all, the book is a great insight into what motivated Australian explorers in the 19th century and it's a top read, particularly if you're out camping in the Pilbara and you're able to imagine what it must have been like back in "the bad old days".

**Right:** The Bungarra Lizard

**Right**: Heading north (well,
sort of) from Nullagine.

"We were about to intrude into the lives of the last nomadic people in the Western Gibson Desert and in doing so it was possible that we might be responsible for bringing to an end, a way of life that had gone on for several thousand years."

*- W. J. Peasley*

# The Last of the Nomads

A fascinating account of an expedition into the Gibson desert to find Warri and Yatungka, the last of the desert nomads.

Mudjon, one of the elders of the Mandildjara people, leads a rescue party into the desert to recover the couple, who are feared dead after consecutive droughts.

An excellent insight into the relationship nomadic Aborigines have for their land and the hardships they endured. Warri's face says it all.

120 pages. Published by Fremantle Arts Centre Press. Available through Pilbara Tourist Bureaus.

There's an entertaining yarn circulating the Pilbara about the white, government consultant who flew in to an Aboriginal community in the Western Desert to address the elders about a multi-million dollar government project to help their community. He spoke articulately and enthusiastically for several hours about it being a "new pilot project" and the benefits it would bring to the region in terms of roads, housing, water and electricity.

Throughout his address the elders nodded encouragingly until the consultant wound up his speech, packed his briefcase and flew back to Perth. As he boarded the plane, one community leader overheard him patting himself on the back and saying how impressed he was that the group had grasped the essence of his address.

Shortly after the plane had taken off, one of the elders pulled aside the community leader and said he was particularly encouraged by what the white fella had to say.

"We could do with a pilot round here," he said.

..." I wonder how we'll go getting a plane?"

One of the many picturesque waterholes along
the Skull Springs Road, near Nullagine.

# BUSH TUCKER

**I** knew there was reason for concern the minute he gutted the wild turkey and instead on throwing the bird on the coals of the fire, he threw the gizzards on and put the turkey in the back of my car for later.

"We like our food a bit raw," he said rolling the entrails in the ashes with a branch before handing some to me on a bush plate of green twigs (out of courtesy, I think, he left my portion on a little longer). Entree, I presume!

It was actually quite tasty (though, in an uncharacteristic gesture of selflessness, I insisted he have the lion's share of the remaining organs).

**Left** and **Right:** Bush tucker delicacies - - Wild turkey and sweet flowers.

And so began one of the highlights of my foray into "Bush Tucker" in the Pilbara, a two day excursion along the fringe of the Western Desert with two Aboriginal elders. It was a rare opportunity, as a Western Desert community was exploring the possibility of becoming involved in tourism and I had been invited to assess the prospect of the community hosting bush tucker tours, producing handicrafts for tourists and providing an insight into the culture of the Western Desert people. During the two days we drove around and sucked on an assortment of deliciously sweet yellow flowers. We chomped on a tasty slug from inside a "bush coconut",

dug up and nibbled on the moist roots of an abundant purple flower and located some bush potatoes and honey ants. We followed a few tracks - lizards, kangaroos and snakes, all edible - and located water by digging up soaks in a dry river bed. That night I sat by the campfire and was told stories about the heavens and how

the land was formed. Pointing upward, one of my hosts outlined a giant emu in a constellation. Having been told of how one of the elders had survived six months in the desert when cut off by flood, I expected him to gather a mattress of spinifex, maybe curl up next to a log to sleep. Instead, in a scene reminiscent of Crocodile Dundee, he pulled a collapsible bed and mattress off the roof rack and suggested that if I wanted to rough it the traditional way that was up to me. He, on the other hand, was planning for a good night's sleep. The next day we drove to The Seven Sisters, a series of waterholes well known to Aborigines. I must have misunderstood, I thought he said they were just 20 minutes away. We travelled for three hours. While my passenger's English was substantially better than my Mardu, we drove along in a silence he didn't appear to find awkward. It was not long before we left the dirt road and headed off into the bush. "Follow the track," said my host. For the life of me, I couldn't see one. "That way, follow the track," he reiterated. Hand signals soon replaced his words (left, right, straight and, a strange one, which I painfully learned was watch out for the hole). Eventually we arrived. As I pointed out on alighting from the car, if I'd had to get back on my own, this would have been the end of me. How he found his way to this largely flat, nondescript location after driving off into the bush three hours ago, I had absolutely no idea. The site of the seven small rock waterholes, we were told, was a significant Corroboree and meeting place for many traditional Aborigines. It was created when seven sisters roamed the land and camped here. Having heard that Aboriginal people "sing up" the land to replenish it, I asked our hosts if there was a song attached to The Seven Sisters. Both men started singing in language. I presume it was an ancient verse. After a few photos ("Sure, go ahead"), we made a fire which was when the Turkey came in and I subsequently pulled out the old "emergency back up" from the car -- a few loaves of bread and some sliced cheese which we all shared before heading back.

All up, the two days was an interesting and enjoyable insight into the life of the desert nomad, one which left no doubt in my mind about the little understood wealth of traditional Aboriginal people.

As to the likelihood of developing a small-scale tourism business, well, I think I'm safe to say there would be huge demand by tourists for a similar experience, and efforts are being made to realise its potential. But how long it will take to link that demand with a community which is transient by nature and chooses to live a remote existence is anybody's guess. In the meantime, rest assured, the land is in safe hands.

I've tasted life in no man's land,
I've fed the flies outback
I've tramped the empty tucker bags on
Lawson's lonely track.
I've toiled in northern Queensland
where I thought the sun could shine
But no mistake, it takes the cake, this
road to Nullagine

         - *Ted Gregg, 1890*

# THE ROAD TO NULLAGINE

There's something perversely pleasurable about delving into history on your holiday and reliving the hardship of the past in relative comfort. The greater the extremes, the better (well, that's what I reckon, anyway).

So, as you're driving along the dirt road to, or from, Nullagine in your airconditioned car, spare a thought for what it must have been like for the "diggers" (literally) of the 1890s who traipsed the Pilbara in search of gold. To begin, cast your mind back to an Australia which, at the time, was going through the worst depression in its history. Banks had closed their doors, farmers were walking off their land, thousands were out of work, with many men forced to wander the roadways with their swags to earn a few bob to send back to their families or some "tucker" to survive. In a world which must have been rich with despair, suddenly the cry went out: "Gold!" Stories followed of men stubbing their toes on huge nuggets or, as was actually the case just outside of Roebourne, a 15 year old boy who picked up a rock to throw at a crow and found it laden with the rich mineral. Gold fever swept the nation and, with the stories of instant wealth, men in their droves cashed in the last of their meagre savings, jumped on the first ship to the Pilbara and headed inland in search of their fortunes.

As the spinifex hurtles past your car window and clouds of red dust fill your rear vision mirror, think back to the 1890s and imagine yourself among the exodus of hopeful men from the coast who wandered the inland terrain you're now travelling. Consider the hardship. If you were like many others, in your haste to get to the goldfields ahead of the competition, desperation would have clouded your judgement and you would have begun the journey with no real idea of the distance involved or the extremes in temperature. For two weeks you would have been travelling on foot under the blazing sun in 40 degree heat, pushing a heavy wheelbarrow and a few possessions including a pick and a pan. Thirst, hunger and flies would have plagued you constantly. As water was scarce, your body would have been constantly irritated by prickly heat - despite regularly "dry washing" your sweat-soaked clothes. You would have eaten maybe once a day and food would have been limited to damper and "tinned dog" (canned meat).

Along the thin, dusty trail which pointed inland, you would have met others going in the opposite direction, many emaciated and broken, some having not even reached the goldfields. Those who did make it would have shared tales of hardship and suffering. Endless days of back-breaking work in exhaustive heat for nothing or, at best, a few specks of alluvial gold -- just enough to go on, while others died from hunger and exhaustion. But for you still fresh with the despair of the past, there would be no turning back. Sleep on the hard, unforgiving earth or on a hessian sack strung between two boughs would have been the only escape from the uncertainly of your endeavour... Phew, they were hard times.

If nothing else, a quick peek into the past and the opportunity to experience the landscape for yourself certainly makes you appreciate the times we're living in today. Enjoy your drive!

**WARNING**

NO– FOOD, WATER OR FUEL
AVAILABLE BEYOND THIS POINT
BEFORE YOU PROCEED –

1. HAVE YOU CHECKED ROAD CONDITIONS ?
2. IS YOUR VEHICLE SUITABLY EQUIPPED ?
3. DO YOU HAVE SUFFICIENT FOOD, WATER AND FUEL ?
4. DO YOU KNOW THE AREA YOU ARE ENTERING ?
5. HAVE YOU NOTIFIED NULLAGINE POLICE OF YOUR INTENDED MOVEMENTS ?

IF IN DOUBT, DO NOT PROCEED BEYOND THIS POINT!
INSTEAD, SEEK ADVICE FROM THE POLICE AT NULLAGINE

DO NOT– BE NUMBERED AMONGST THOSE WHO HAVE PERISHED
IN THIS AREA DUE TO THE LACK OF PREPAREDNESS

**Above**: A sound warning for the intrepid traveller.
**Right:** The reflective pools of Marble Bar. **Next Page**:
A panoramic view over Marble Bar.

# Marble Bar

Sadly, my first visit to Marble Bar is likely to have moved into the realms of folklore, at least in the minds of one unsuspecting group of people who happened to be there at the same time I was.

I had arrived in February as part of my orientation of the region, at a time when the town lived up to its reputation of being the hottest in Australia (the dubious title was awarded following 160 consecutive days where the mercury rose above 100 degrees Fahrenheit or 37 degrees Celsius). I had driven all morning and decided to head for the nearest waterhole for a swim. Past Chinaman Pool on the Coongan River, I arrived at Marble Bar Pool around midday. Understandably, there was no one around (45 degrees does that to you) and, feeling brave, I decided to drop my drawers and go skinny dipping, reasoning that few tourists were around at this time of year and that my clothing would be within easy reach in an emergency. It must have been sometime between noting the mirrored effect of my toes poking through the surface of the water and my fascination with the streaks of jasper in the rock, that I drifted beyond what I would have considered to be safe distance of my pants and heard the rumbling of a vehicle just over the hill. Panic. A frantic swim, I concluded, would see me arriving too late; the only option left was to sprint. While my desperate departure from the brackish water of the pool was far from flattering, much less complimentary was my comic attempt to cover the 50m of blazing sand that separated me from my shorts. Particularly ungainly, I suspect, was that half way into my mad dash, my seriously seared feet decided to abandon my body's trajectory and head for a small island of brown grass and leaves which promised some respite.

Which was about when the busload of geriatric tourists ground to a halt. Suffice to say, it was not a good look. A stark naked man precariously poised on one foot on the bank of a remote creek bed clinging to his "Marbles" in 45 degree heat.

My only consolation was that after everyone had taken their photos, one kind gentleman - probably still laughing to this day - reunited me with my clothes before departing.

I was born black
When I'm cold I'm black
When I'm scared I'm black
When I'm sunburnt I'm black
When I'm sick I'm black
And when I die I'm black
You were born white
When you're cold you're blue
When you're scared you're yell
When you're sunburnt you're r
When you're sick you're green
and when you die you're grey

......and you've got the hide
     to call me coloured!

- Stuck up on a board at the Ironclad
  Hotel, Marble Bar

Coppins Gap

# Marble Bar to Coppins Gap

This is a highly recommended day trip or overnight stop about an hour and a half's drive from Marble Bar. A two wheel drive would make the journey fairly easily, assuming rains haven't caused havoc with the roads. Go out of Marble Bar along the sealed road for about 9km and turn left towards Port Hedland. Then on for another 40km or so and chuck a right at Woodie Woodie road. (You can see Coppins Gap in the distance). Veer right on Bamboo Creek road, follow it for about 10 km and turn left. First left is Kitty's Gap, straight on is Coppins Gap. The best time of year to visit is around Easter or after there has been a bit of rain. What makes it special is walking through the canyon of deep red jasper (nothing like Marble Bar where the jasper is more white and blue). You'll see two steep walls of twisted patterned jasper with some pleasant swimming holes in between.

**Hint:** Throw water on the jasper to bring out the richness and patterns of the rock.

# Port Hedland

# Port Hedland

There are some people who would say that, in terms of appearance, Port Hedland is a baby only a mother could love. Hot, dry and stained pink by the red dust of the huge BHP iron ore processing plant, it's a harbour town often associated with impressions of mangy vacant lots and forlorn fibro houses with cyclone-proof windows. In tourism terms, say many who have passed through, "Why would anyone want to go to Hedland?"

Well, I think we can safely say the secret's out: Port Hedland is not your Gold Coast type tourist town -- but then, the fact is, it's never pretended to be. It's a working town - a transient, work hard/play hard, community with its own unique character that revolves around Australia's largest export industry -- mining. And that's what makes it interesting. Forget, for a moment, the palm trees and the pristine white sands you can see elsewhere and think about this nation's resource industry and the engineering feats involved in moving and processing millions of tonnes of iron ore which later becomes the cars we drive and the roof over our heads. And it's accessible. Where else can you deviate 10 minutes

**Far Right:** A giant Bucket Wheel Reclaimer used to transfer the iron ore.

off the highway and see a train that's nearly three kilometres - 240 carriages - in length? Where else can you tour a processing plant where you can see 65 tonnes of carriage loaded with 180 tonnes of ore tipped upside down to relieve it of its cargo in minutes? Where else can you stand alongside a ship that dwarfs anything else on the water and marvel at the massive structures that have been created to transport mountains of processed iron ore into hulls that will take it around the world. And throughout it all you'll hear facts and figures which you'll still be trying to relate to some time later when you're lying on that pristine beach. Consider, for example, that the trains you have seen move more than 71 million tons of iron ore a year from the inland Pilbara. Seven trips a day, 364 days of the year. At about 28,000 tonnes a trip, that's about $3 million a day (give or take a few variations and my atrocious numerical skills). Not a bad little earner. And, here's one that fascinated me (no mean feat as details of all things mechanical tend to go in one ear and out the other). There are about 2,000 wheels on each train, all of which are checked by an x-ray monitor sitting next to the rail that can detect a hairline fault as it appears in any one wheel -- while the train is moving!

Well, I was impressed.

So if you're into mining, technology or just all things big, a 10 minute deviation through a north-west "working town" and a tour of the BHP operation in Port Hedland is an interesting way to spend half a day.

For more information check with the Port Hedland Tourist Bureau.

147

# NaCl.....salt

It's been referred to as "The world's biggest cocaine deposit" and "The only ski slope you'll find in 40 degree heat" but let me assure you, the last thing you'd want to do is suck it up through your nose or fall on it. It's salt ( is that NaCl?) though industrial salt as opposed to the one on your kitchen table which is much more refined) and it's piled as high as a mountain waiting to get shipped around the world for use in making plastics, chrome, glass and chemicals.

It's one of the first things you see when you drive into Port Hedland.

According to those in the know, the salt takes about 24 months to "grow". The process basically involves letting in the salt water from the Indian Ocean and allowing it to dry from the sun in huge ponds before harvesting it. The different colours of the pond (refer previous photo) represent different stages in the evaporative process. In Port Hedland, the Cargill Salt expanse covers about 7,800 hectares which are divided into 28 ponds that exchange water from one to the other until the water has completely evaporated and the sodium chloride proportion has increased from 17% to 90% (are you impressed?). The salt is then collected by harvesters and trucks, cleaned and processed into the stockpile before being transferred to the waiting ships.

And a few facts to "pepper"(sorry) your holiday...

-The salt layer is about 30cm deep when it's harvested.

- In a 18 hour day, the site harvests about 16-18,000 tonnes of salt.

- The bulldozers on top of the salt mounds work around the clock when the ships are in.

- The ships carry about 40,000 tonnes of salt.

- Each truck towing three trailer is moving 92 tonnes of salt.

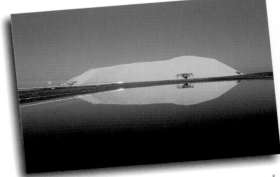

**Previous Page** and **Right**: The salt lakes and salt stockpile at Port Hedland

Once a year outside the infamous Pier Hotel in Port Hedland a strange ritual takes place involving bikies, beer and a huge cloud of rubber smoke.

The objective - according to those in the know - is to spin the back wheel of your motorbike until the tyre "blows out". The prize - determined by the applause of the surrounding crowd - is a new tyre. The catch: There's a heap of contestants and only one tyre to be won!

Well, it appeared to make sense to the enthusiastic participants, and if you're around Port Hedland in early August and you're into motorbikes, rock and roll, tatts and the odd drink, the Hedland Riders Annual Bike Show is worth a look in. The weekend is bigger than Ben Hur, with locals, bikies ("Yeah, we had the Coffin Cheaters up from Perth this year, 25 of them followed up by 35 police cars") converging at the Pier Hotel for a weekend of serious socialising.

On the two-day program: Two rock bands, some topless dancers, a wet T-shirt and tattoo competition and the eagerly awaited Burn out Competition. For the uninitiated, the rider secures the front wheel of his bike into a specially made corral, then revs his motor and drops the clutch so his back wheel spins. Within minutes, the tyre heats up, heaps of smoke billows from the back, burning rubber shrapnel spins off into the air and, eventually, the tyre explodes -- much to the appreciative roar of the drunken and blackened faced crowd. The appeal of the event: At the risk of upsetting a Harley rider, "If I have to explain it, you wouldn't understand".

# Station Stays

Station stays are a relatively new concept in tourism and a great way to learn more about the area you're travelling through. It's good for "the cockies" as it supplements their income when times are tough, and it's fun for tourists who get a real taste of what country life in the area is all about. Station stays or farm stays can vary, though one thing's for sure: you can forget your uniformed concierge meeting you at the door. Instead, you're likely to be greeted by a dusty owner and a bit of good old country hospitality. Some offer a bed and a roof over your head, while others provide the opportunity to stay in the homestead and virtually become part of the family. Generally speaking though, you can expect good value for money, an insight into pastoral life and the chance to meet some friendly, down to earth, people. My advice: Pull into a local tourist bureau and ask for details about station stays in the area.

# Pardoo Station

(About an hour and a half north of Port Hedland)

The first time I spoke with Pam Leeds of Pardoo Station she was about to host a bus-load of German tourists who had stepped off a ship in Port Hedland and were travelling north for lunch to experience some true "nor-west hospitality". Just before the ship berthed, the travel agent organising the group had rung her to say the Germans were very particular and that they would expect silver service and wine with their meal. Well, Pam told the agent - in no uncertain terms - that that was not what Pardoo was all about, that the food would be served on paper plates as it always had been and that in 40 degree heat, she had no intention of serving wine for lunch. The result: The Germans came anyway and thought lunch at Pardoo Station was the highlight of their trip. Photographs, videos, farewell songs, the lot. The travel agent later rang to apologise. Pardoo Station is a half million acre cattle

**Left:** Cape Keraudren, near Pardoo Station.

153

property (Santa Gertrudis stud) which is bordered by the west coast. A 15km drive off the North-West Coastal Highway down a good unsealed road sees you at the homestead - a National Trust Building - which was built in the 1860s. The homestead typifies the design of pastoral homes built in the Pilbara during that era. Made of stone and mortar, the building has a square core of several large rooms with no passages or a main entrance hall, a corrugated roof with three meter ceilings and verandas on all sides. Huge iron cyclone shutters are hinged at the roof line. The kitchen and dining room are separate from the main house and several corrugated tin worksheds have been built nearby.

For visiting travellers, there is a range of accommodation (though, understandably, Pam and her husband John have kept the homestead for themselves). You can choose from several simple rooms (dongas) with air conditioning, a small house which can be rented by a family, powered sites (with a shower block) and a shaded area for camping. Pam also runs a small shop which provides bait (Pardoo's repeat business is testament to the good fishing to be had), frozen food packs and drinks, all of which are reasonably priced. And there's a rustic swimming pool made in the 1960s from local rock which is fed continually from an artesian bore.

For things to do: Well, sitting in the shade or by the pool with a good book is a good start, but for the more active you can scatter the cattle and head off across the station to Mount Blaze (previously the site of a lighthouse) or wander across to the islands at low tide. Both are pleasant half-day excursions. Pam provides mud maps and, if you're into birds, visiting birdwatchers from the Royal Australian Ornithological Union have identified about 80 different species which visit Pardoo, including the huge White bellied Sea Eagle, of which I saw three during my visit. All up, it's a relaxing - and reasonably priced - overnight visit and a handy respite from the long drive between Port Hedland and Broome.

The north-west coast of Western Australia experiences more severe cyclones than any other part of the Australian coastline, and it is one of the most cyclone-prone coasts anywhere in the world.

On average, two cyclones cross the Western Australian coast each cyclone season (between November and April).

While the chances of being hit by a cyclone are slim, if you see the skies darkening, best tune into the radio just to make sure.

I was in Port Hedland when Cyclone Rachel passed over with winds of about 170km/h. The "eye" was fun (dead still and a chance to compare notes with the neighbours), though the tempest on either side of it was a bit worrying.

The best part about it was that by the end, everyone else's garden looked like mine had all year!

# 80 Mile B

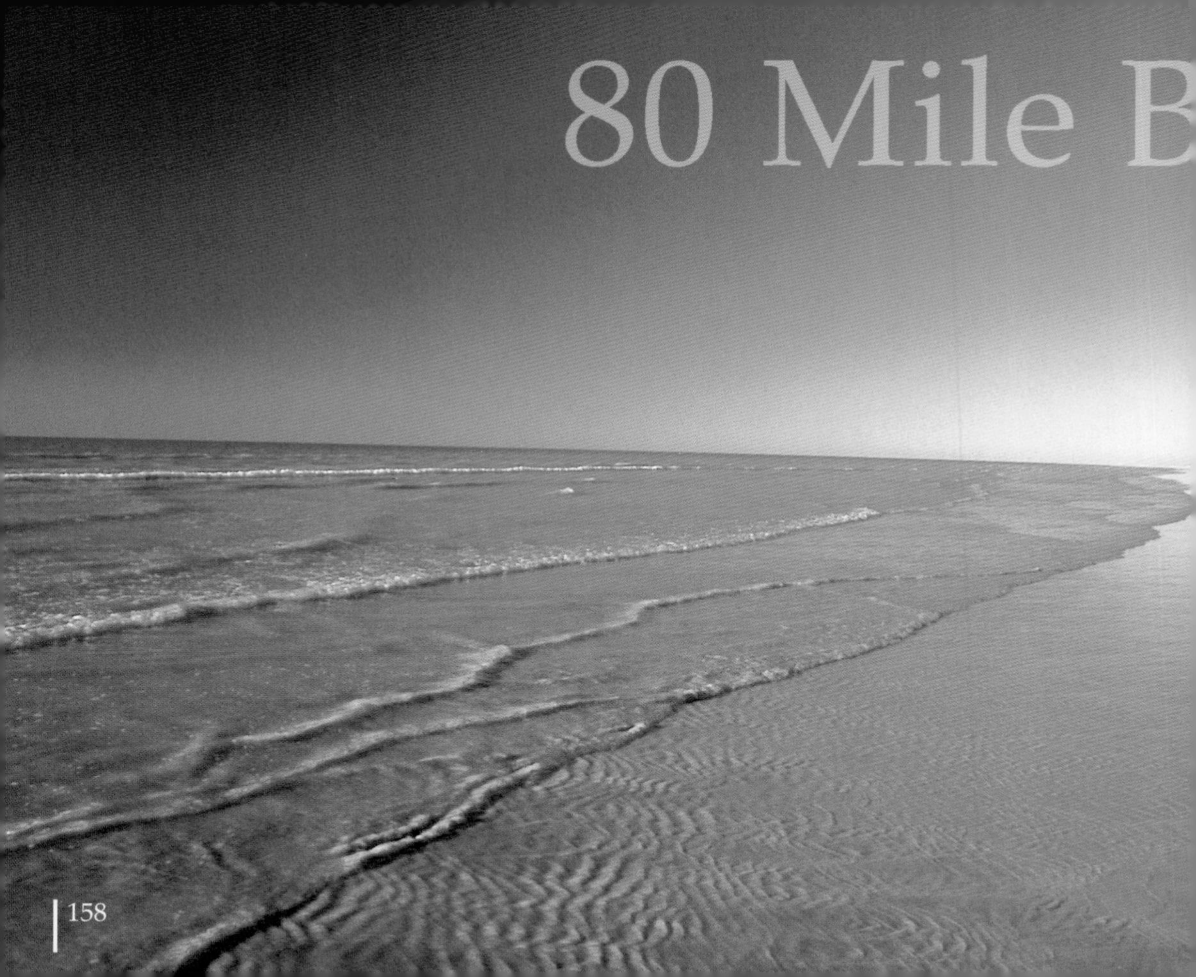

ach

For those heading north, Cape Keraudren is the beginning of 80 Mile Beach, a sprawling coastline of white sand and turquoise waters.

The Cape is a popular spot for southern fishermen migrating north for the winter so in peak season expect to see communities of caravans, dinghies and small power boats huddled around the best sites. There are powered sites and toilets; check with the ranger on your way in. Everything else is bring your own. Most people tend to stay to the south of the creek estuary but if you like the idea of taking your car along the beach and finding that idyllic private spot, wait until the tide drops and you're away (Big tip: Get a tide chart or you could end up stranded for several hours waiting to cross some of the creeks.) If you want to see Cape Keraudren at its best, plan to arrive on high tide. The water looks great and the sand's white and clean. The edge of the estuary is a pleasant place for a picnic and it's safe for kids. Otherwise, the 7m tidal range gives you a fair bit of room to drive north along the beach and find somewhere to camp. If you collect shells, wait until just after a storm to head up the beach. You'll find thousands of them. Birds are also a big drawcard along the Pilbara Coast as the huge tidal range and plentiful food draw migratory birds from all over the world.

**Previous Page and Above:** 80 Mile Beach
**Right:** "The Office"

## Published books in the Pocket Guide Series

- The Pocket Guide to The Red Centre.
- The Pocket Guide to Western Australia's Pilbara Region
- The Pocket Guide to the Top End
- The Pocket Guide to Western Australia's Kimberley Region

## To order

Contact Hema Maps
PO Box 4365 Eight Mile Plains
Brisbane, Queensland Australia. 4113
Ph: 61 7 3340 0000
Fax: 61 7 3340 0099
E-mail: manager@hemamaps.com.au
www.hemamaps.com

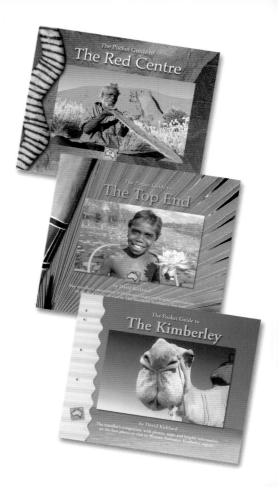

# Index of place names and prominent features

## Photo Credits and Technical Acknowledgements

There are several outstanding photographs I've used in this book for which I would like to acknowledge **Simon Westlake**. Simon was commissioned by the Pilbara Tourism Association during my stewardship and joined Creative Director **Vaughan Sutherland** and myself on an intense five-day photo shoot of four main Pilbara sites ("Never again," says Vaughan, who still wakes in a cold sweat with flashbacks of the ordeal). Simon's photos appear on pages 71,10,67,73,81,95,102.

The photograph on page 75 was drawn from the Australian Tourism Commission's library. Woodside and BHP photographs used in relevant stories have been provided by the companies. The photograph on page 22 was taken by **Col Roberts** and the photograph on page 77 was taken by **Chris Muller**. The excellent whale shark and manta ray photos on page 17 and 18 were taken by **Ron Campbell.**

It would be fair to say this book may never have looked this good if it were not for the support of **Tim Nemeth,** from TT Digital in Brisbane who scanned all of my images and provided desperately needed technical advice throughout the production phase of the project and **Trefor Smith,** from Kingswood Press, who painstakingly ensured the quality of my transparencies was transferred to the book. I'd also like to thank Chris Muller from CALM and each of the tourist bureau managers who took the time to proof read the book to ensure its accuracy: Kirsty, Duncan, Linda,Phil and Robbie.

To each of you, my gratitude and sincere thanks. It's been fun working with you.

# The Author

David Kirkland is a full-time travel writer and photographer specialising in Australia, South-east Asia and the South Pacific. A journalist, photographer and author with more than 10 years experience in the tourism industry, he travelled the world extensively before settling in Brisbane, Queensland. The Pocket Guide to The Pilbara is one of four books in the series. David has also written and photographed several other books. His coffee table book Impressions of Papua New Guinea is considered essential reading for anyone visiting the country. He has also published a stable of travel and photographic souvenir publications on destinations in the region. David can be contacted by email directly on: frontierpub@bigpond.com.au.

## SOME HELPFUL PHONE NUMBERS

Cyclone Warning Movements 1300 659 210
National Parks Regional Headquarters: (08) 9143 1488
Karijini National Park Ranger: (08) 9189 8157
Millstream National Park Ranger: (08) 9184 5144
Road Condition Report (Main Roads): 1800 013 314
Police (Regional Western Australia): (08) 9222 1649

## VISITORS CENTRES

| | |
|---|---|
| Exmouth: | (08) 9949 1176 |
| Onslow: | (08) 9184 6644 |
| Karratha: | (08) 9144 4600 |
| Roebourne: | (08) 9182 1060 |
| Port Hedland: | (08) 9173 1711 |
| Tom Price: | (08) 9188 1112 |
| Newman: | (08) 9175 2888 |

The Pocket Guide

Travel Book Series

# INDY 500
## THE INSIDE TRACK

by Nancy Roe Pimm

DARBY
CREEK
PUBLISHING

Published by Darby Creek Publishing,
a division of Oxford Resources, Inc.
7858 Industrial Parkway
Plain City, OH 43064
www.darbycreekpublishing.com

Text copyright © 2004 by Nancy Roe Pimm
Illustrations © 2004 by Darby Creek Publishing
Design by Keith Van Norman

Cataloging-in-Publication

Pimm, Nancy Roe.
Indy 500 : the inside track / by Nancy Roe
Pimm.
        p. ; cm.
ISBN 1-58196-021-2 hardcover
ISBN 1-58196-023-9 softcover
Summary: A look at the history and excitement
of "the Crown Jewel" of auto racing, the
Indianapolis 500, including the history of the
Indianapolis Motor Speedway and the develop-
ment of "Indy cars."—Includes bibliographical
references (p. ) and index.
1. Indianapolis Speedway Race—Juvenile litera-
ture. 2. Automobile racing—Indiana—
Indianapolis—Juvenile literature. [1. Indianapolis
Speedway Race. 2. Automobile racing—
Indiana—Indianapolis. 3. Indy cars.] I. Title.
GV1033.5.I55 P56 2004
796.72/06/877252 dc22
OCLC: 54012992

Printed in the United States of America

First printing

2 4 6 8 10 9 7 5 3 1

*Every year the Borg-Warner Trophy is awarded to the newest Indy 500 champion. Each winner's face, name, and winning year are permanently placed on it. The trophy also features a 24-karat-gold portrait of the late Speedway owner, Anton "Tony" Hulman. An 18-inch replica, a "Baby Borg," is given each year to the Indy 500 champion and the car owner.*

# TABLE OF CONTENTS

START
YOUR
ENGINES!

Every May, drivers from all over the world come to Indianapolis, Indiana, to test their skills. Their race cars know no nationality, race, or gender. They will go as fast as they are pushed to go. Every team races by the same rules: The car must be sixteen feet long and six-feet, six-and-a-half-inches wide. It must weigh at least 1,525 pounds, not counting the fuel or the driver.

Each driver puts on his or her race face. Calculating eyes peering through helmet, showing steely determination. Strapped into a rocket-like car, the driver is about to travel at speeds of more than 200 miles per hour, just inches off the ground with cement walls looming beside him.

The drivers line up three cars wide and eleven rows deep. After a lifetime of dreams and a month of intense preparation, the next Indy 500 champion will be decided in one afternoon. The drivers await a single command:

"Lady and gentlemen, start your engines!"

# TRACK OF DREAMS

In the early 1900s, former racecar driver Carl Fisher had visions of building a test track. Along with three partners—Arthur Newby, Frank Wheeler, and Jim Allison—Mr. Fisher bought 320 acres of overgrown farmland northwest of Indianapolis, Indiana. In those days, Indianapolis—not Detroit—was "Motor City." Construction of the track began in February 1909.

By August 1909, Fisher's dream came true. A 2.5-mile, oval-shaped racetrack stood where there once had been only a cornfield. Four banked corners connected two long straightaways (5/8 mile each) and two short straightaways (1/8 mile each). The partners named their track of dreams the Indianapolis Motor Speedway.

The first race was set for August 19, 1909. Racecar drivers from all over the country came to test their cars and compete against each other

*Winter 1909: Lewis Strang, who would become the pole-sitter in the 1911 Indy 500, checks out a model of the soon-to-be-constructed track.*

*(left to right) Tom Kincade #6, Charlie Merz #7, and William Borque #3
at the start of the track's first race on August 19, 1909.*

that day. The tires on the "high-speed" cars tore up the track's crushed stone and tar surface. Five people died because of the poor track conditions.

Fisher decided to have the track repaved before opening for another race. Two months later, 3.2 million ten-pound bricks had been laid, held together with cement. Since then, the Indianapolis Motor Speedway has been known throughout the world as "the Brickyard." In 1911 the first Indy 500 was held.

The racecars kept getting faster and faster. The cars hammered away at the bricks, and they eventually broke apart, too. At first the Speedway workers patched the spots that needed repair. By the 1930s, most of the track needed to be covered with blacktop. The track was completely covered in October 1961, after the race's 50th anniversary. A 36-inch strip of bricks was left uncovered at the start/finish line, just to remind everyone how the nickname "Brickyard" began.

*Tony Hulman (left), with Ray Harroun, 1911 Winner (right) on the "yard of bricks," celebrates the 50-year anniversary in 1961.*

# THE RACE

In 1909 and 1910, several short races were held at the "Brickyard." But in 1911, the Speedway became the home of only one race a year: The Indianapolis 500.

The first Indianapolis 500 was held on Memorial Day, May 30, 1911. Forty-six drivers from the United States and Europe came to compete for a purse of $27,550. Ninety thousand fans poured into the grandstands. They cheered on the forty drivers who had qualified for the big race.

The cars lined up in eight rows of five across. At the drop of the flag, the drivers took off and circled the track two hundred times. When the race was over, the winner's car had averaged 74.6 miles per hour. It took more than seven hours for all of the cars to finish the race!

*First race at the Indianapolis Motor Speedway, 1909*

Since that day, the Indianapolis 500 has become the Super Bowl of auto racing. On each Memorial Day weekend, between 300,000 and 350,000 fans spill through the gates. More than 325 million households watch the race on television all over the world. The Indy 500 boasts the largest crowds of any single sporting event in the world.

Preparations for the race begin the first weekend of May, when the race teams pull into the track. They spend the month taking practice laps and getting ready to qualify for the race. The

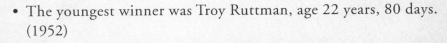

## INDY 500 FAST FACTS

- The slowest average speed was 74.602 mph. (Harroun, 1911)
- The fastest average speed was 185.981 mph. (Luyendyk, 2000)
- Indy-style cars accelerate from 0 to 100 mph in 3 seconds.
- Every time an Indy driver blinks, he misses 50 feet of track.
- The youngest winner was Troy Ruttman, age 22 years, 80 days. (1952)
- The oldest winner was Al Unser, age 47 years, 360 days. (1987)
- A front tire for an Indy-style car weighs about 18 lbs.
- Some drivers and fans believe that eating peanuts at the track is bad luck.

Thirty-three engines roar behind the pace car as the Indy-style cars roll down the track. The drivers wave to their fans during the two parade laps. They zig-zag their cars over the pavement to warm up their tires. On the third lap—the pace lap—the cars pick up speed. It's time to get down to business. The drivers await the signal from the starter, perched high above the track. The green flag waves wildly and the race is on!

The cars scream into the first turn, ducking and diving. Five hundred miles later, when the first car passes under the checkered flag, the race is over. Then comes the celebration. The winning driver chugs the traditional drink—milk. A large wreath is placed around his neck. A new Indianapolis 500 winner is crowned.

## THE DRINK OF CHAMPIONS

*2003 Winner Gil de Ferran*

Louis Meyer's mom once told him that milk was the most refreshing drink of all. After Louie won the 1936 Indy 500, he celebrated in the winner's circle by drinking—not champagne—but a bottle of buttermilk! To this day, the milk-drinking tradition continues at Indy.

# THE CARS

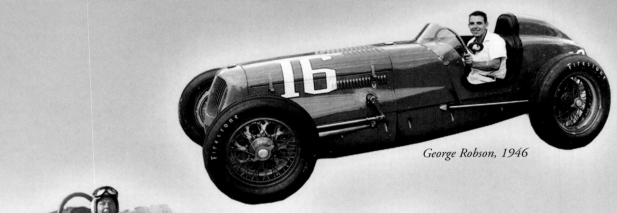

*George Robson, 1946*

*Ray Crawford, 1959*

*A.J. Foyt IV, 2003*

In the early 1900s, the Indy racecars looked like farm tractors with tall, narrow tires. They were made of rigid steel frames covered by heavy sheet-metal bodies. The two-seater, front-engine machines had to weigh at least 2,300 pounds. The skies filled with smoke as noisy engines powered the heavy racecars through the turns and down the straightaways.

The two-seater cars held a driver and a riding mechanic. The mechanic's job was to keep the car running and to watch for passing traffic. Ray Harroun was the only driver in the first Indy 500 to drive without a mechanic. He designed a single-seater racecar and kept track of his pursuers with the use of a mirror mounted in front of the steering wheel on the body of the car. This is the first recorded use of a rearview mirror.

rearview mirror →

Ray Harroun's
1911 "Marmon Wasp"

Harroun was ahead of his time. The car he designed was also lighter and narrower than the other Indy cars in 1911. It had a hornet-like tail that earned it the nickname, "the Marmon Wasp." Ray Harroun and the Marmon Wasp won the first Indy 500. The following year, in 1912, a new rule made it mandatory to have a mechanic ride with the driver. Single-seater cars didn't become legal again until 1923.

*Jules Goux, the winner of the 1913 Indy 500. Car weight: 2200 lbs. Average race speed: 75.933 mph*

It wasn't long before the car builders discovered that the lighter the car, the faster the car. The rearview mirror became standard on the lighter single-seater cars. Instead of using street cars, special lightweight racecars were made for competition. Over the years the Indy-style cars have been made of steel, aluminum, carbon, or a combination of these. Today they have a carbon chassis and carbon body work. ("Indy cars" is a nickname given to the style of cars driven at the Indianapolis 500.) They became so light and fast that the drivers had trouble keeping them under control. At high speeds, the cars tended to lift off the track!

*Juan Montoya, winner of the 2000 Indianapolis 500. Car weight: 1550 lbs. Average race speed: 167.607 mph*

In 1971, a new design showed up among the race teams. The new Indy-style cars had two sets of wings: a set in front on the nose of the car and a large wing on the rear.

By 1979 engineers created cars that used a suction called "ground effects." Air flows by the front wings and into the tunnels underneath the car to hold the front end down. The suction that is created this way makes a 1,550-pound car hug the ground like a 3,875-pound car. Someone could actually drive one of these cars on a ceiling! At a street race in Detroit, the Indy-style cars sucked up the manhole covers as they raced over them!

The rear wing of the racecar is like an upside-down airplane wing. Instead of creating lift as on an airplane, the wing pushes the

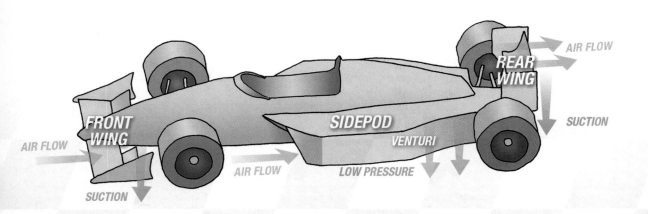

*Today's Indy-style cars can travel the length of a football field in less than one second!*

car down onto the track. This is called "downforce," like when a person's hand pushes down on a toy car. The air is forced up and over the racecar, which is called "aerodynamics." The wings give the drivers more control of the car. The faster the car travels, the tighter it hugs the track. The drivers rocket through the turns so fast that it almost seems as if they're flying!

Indy champ Bobby Rahal says, "The easiest laps I ever did at Indy were the fastest laps I ever did at Indy The faster you go, the better it feels. I've been in cars going slower around Indy and it scared the daylights out of me. I was on the edge, skating around for the entire lap."

# THE ENGINE

The heart of the racecar is the engine. If it stops ticking, the race is over. Today most Indy-style cars are powered by an 8-cylinder, 3.0-liter methanol-fueled engine. It produces more than 675 horsepower, about four times the horsepower of a street car. Driving an Indy car around only one lap of the Brickyard (2.5 miles) is as hard on the engine as going five hundred miles in a passenger car.

Street car engines run at 2,500 to 3,500 r.p.m. (revolutions per minute). An Indy-style car runs at 10,300 r.p.m. Each piston pumps up and down at a rate of about one mile a minute. This makes a

*Working on Sam Hornish's engine.*

Before World War II, Indy racers drove front-engine cars. After some experimentation—and a lot of trial and error—race teams in the 1960s gradually switched to cars with rear engines. Putting the engine in the rear gave the car more balance, so it was easier to handle. This also allowed the front of the car to be smaller and narrower, making the entire car more aerodynamic—and faster.

An Indy 500 car team will go through an average of four engines for each car during the month of May. The engine needs to be rebuilt every 550 miles. It takes an Indy crew about one hour to change an engine.

**23**

# GASOLINE BANNED AT INDY

*Fuel intake, called a "buckeye"*

Gasoline was used for many years, but it is very flammable. When Dave MacDonald's car hit a wall during the 1964 Indianapolis 500, the gas tank exploded, causing a fatal, fiery crash. As a result, the use of gasoline was outlawed.

race engine use a lot of fuel. An Indy-style car engine gets two miles to the gallon. It can burn two gallons of fuel per minute! One lap around the Speedway uses about 1.3 gallons of fuel, which today is methanol, not gasoline.

Methanol is an alcohol-based fuel that is less flammable than gasoline. The only problem with using methanol is that its flame is invisible. The crew can feel the heat but can't see the flame. Instead, they hear the fuel ignite, much like the sound of a gas grill starting. Buckets of water are kept in the pits in case of an accidental fire.

The tank of an Indy-style car is called a fuel cell. It holds 30 gallons of fuel and is located between the driver and the engine. A strong fuel cell is needed to keep down the threat of fire. The fuel cell is similar to the ones used in military helicopters. It is so strong that it can withstand machine-gun fire.

Each Indy 500 car team is allotted 245 gallons of methanol before the start of the race. If a team uses more than the allotted 245 gallons, the car will run out of fuel and won't be able to finish the race. That is no way to lose!

## THE ROAR OF THE ENGINE

The fuel cell is the only thing between the driver's head and the engine. In Ed Pimm's first Indianapolis 500 in 1985, he forgot to put in his earplugs. For more than three hours, the engine screamed in his ears. After the race, he was nearly deaf.

"I got caught up in all the pre-race excitement," says Ed Pimm. "Before I knew it, we were called to our cars. When the green flag dropped and I stood on the throttle, I realized my earplugs were in my pocket. No way was I going to pit just for earplugs! I knew right then that I would have to spend the next 500 miles with this incredible high-pitched whining sound in my ears."

# THE TIRES

Today's racing tires don't look like the first Indy 500 tires. Back in 1911, the racing tires were very skinny, like bicycle tires. They were made of cotton cords covered with a layer of rubber. Blowouts were common—and very dangerous.

Over time, racing tires changed. They became safer and helped racers drive faster. Race teams found that the wider the tire, the more grip the racecar had. When a car has grip, its wheels stay in good contact with the track's surface. Drivers have more control, especially around the turns. Compared to regular tires, racing tires need to provide more traction and grip, so they have to be softer than tires on passenger cars.

Indy-style racing tires look as if they have no tread. They look smooth and bald, so they are called "slicks." Slicks do have tread, but it is flat, not grooved. These tires only work well on dry surfaces. If it rains before or during the Indy 500, the race is postponed until the track is dry.

*patch*
*(area that touches the track)*

*Tires before the race*

**27**

Another factor for good tire grip is heat. When racing tires are heated up, they become sticky like chewing gum. The racecars weave back and forth across the track while waiting for the race to start to make the tires hotter. Then they will stick to the track surface better.

Heat can also be an enemy of the tire. Tire engineers and racing teams work very hard to find a tire that is soft enough to produce lots of traction without blistering or overheating. A tire that swells and pops at over 200 m.p.h. will spell D-I-S-A-S-T-E-R. Tire companies test their tires for durability in laboratories, and they pay drivers per mile to test their products on the racetrack.

*Pit area with tire "peel out" marks.*

These facts will get your wheels turning!

- The tread on an IndyCar Series tire is only slightly thicker than a credit card, 3/32nd of an inch thick.
- The front tire of one of these cars weighs about 18 pounds.
- The temperature of the tread at top speed is almost 212 degrees Farenheit—the boiling point of water.
- At 220 m.p.h. the front tires rotate about 43 times per second.
- The sticking of the tire to the track's surface is called **bite**.
- Bubbles, called **blisters**, sometimes form on the surface of the tire when the tread is overheated.
- To race faster, the drivers use the same groove around the track, which becomes darker because of rubber buildup. The dark area is called the **racing line**. Pieces of rubber get thrown off the tires and collect above the racing line. These are known as **marbles**.
- "Stickers" is a slang term for new tires that still have the manufacturer's stickers on them.
- At the Indy 500, each race team is given 35 sets of tires (140 tires) per team.
- Each tire costs about $300.
- The race teams fill their tires with nitrogen because it doesn't expand or contract as much as oxygen.
- Outer tires (on the right side) are taller than inner tires to give more control through tight turns.
- The actual amount of surface area that the tire's tread touches is called the **tire patch.**

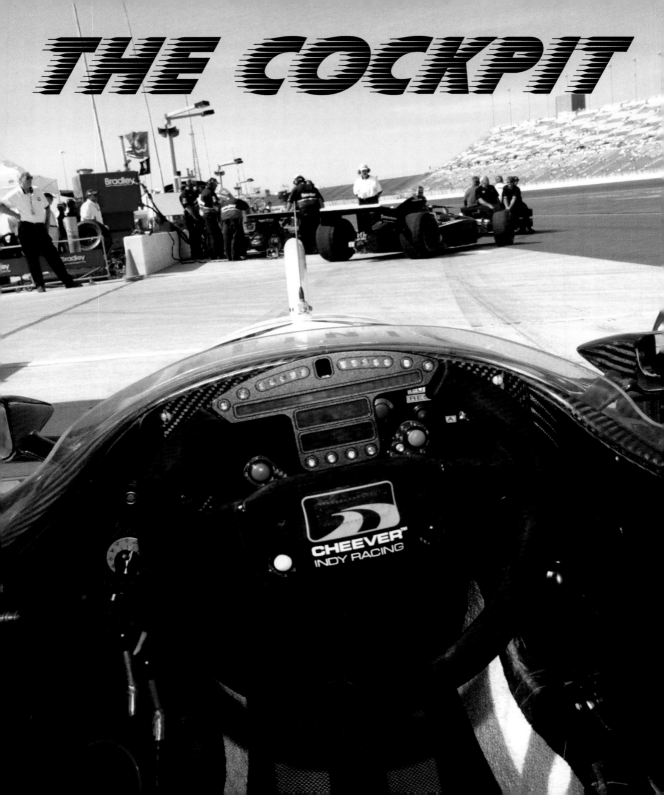

# THE COCKPIT

To step into his office, an Indy 500 driver doesn't have to open any doors. He slides into the cockpit opening, a small 36-by-19-inch area in the middle of the racecar. Mario Andretti says, "When they made the call, 'Drivers, to your cars!' it was such a relief. My racecar was my

*Mario Andretti*

office. It was the place where I felt most relaxed. I had no distractions, and I could be totally focused. I could hardly wait for the green flag to drop so I could get down to business."

The cockpit is so small that teams need to unhook the steering wheel and the headrest in order for the driver to fit. Once the driver is seated, he or she is hooked into place. The driver's seat is an exact mold of his or her body. The racer fits so snugly in the cockpit that a crewmember has to buckle the driver's seatbelt for him. A cockpit is also known as "the tub" or the monocoque. It is made of carbon fiber. This is the same material NASA uses for building rockets in its space program. It also contains Kevlar©, a material used in bullet-proof vests, making the cockpit super-strong to protect the driver.

The long, narrow front of the car is called the nose. Behind the nose and the front tires is the footwell. The gas pedal, brake pedal, clutch pedal, and foot rest are here. The foot rest is a "dead" pedal, used for support around the turns or as a place for the driver to rest his or her foot. Under the driver's legs is a fire extinguisher. One push of a button releases the chemical to put out a fire.

Once the driver is strapped inside the car, he doesn't use a key to start the engine. A crewmember fits the end of a starter into the crankshaft at the rear of the racecar. The starter turns the engine in the same way that a hand-crank did on the Model T Fords.

*Buddy Rice nestled in the cockpit, 2004.*

Unlike a street car with gauges on the dashboard, the Indy-style car has its gauges on the steering wheel. It displays the oil and water temperatures, tire pressures, and the revolutions per minute (r.p.m.s) of the engine. The driver even has an overtake button, which

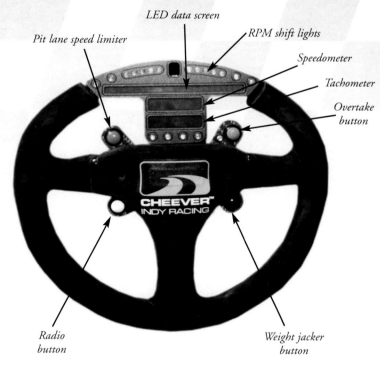

*Pit lane speed limiter*

*LED data screen*

*RPM shift lights*

*Speedometer*

*Tachometer*

*Overtake button*

*Radio button*

*Weight jacker button*

gives the engine more fuel. This gives the car more horsepower to help the driver pass another car. A cruise control button limits the car's speed in the pits to only 60 m.p.h.!

The gearshift in an Indy-style car is similar to that of a motorcycle. The driver simply uses his hand to pull the shifter up when he or she wants to go up a gear—and pushes it down to drop into a lower gear.

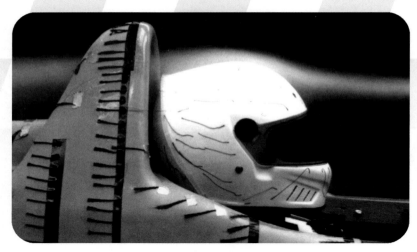

*wind tunnel test*

An Indy car has no roof, so the cockpit is open. The driver must wear a special helmet that not only protects his or her head, but also aerodynamically cuts through the air. At high speeds, a driver used to feel an upward pull of more than fifty pounds on his helmet. The helmet shook violently from side to side, straining the driver's neck muscles and, at times, causing blurred vision. Engineers studied the helmets in wind tunnels, using yarn tufts taped to the helmet and smoke to watch the airflow. The thickly padded helmet they created has a diffuser in the back and a chin spoiler in the front, both making the air run smoothly over the surface of the helmet. The driver has less neck fatigue and fewer vision problems.

Directly behind the driver's head is an air intake opening called an airbox. Air travels into the airbox and is forced into the engine. The rollbar that protects the driver's head is built into the airbox. The Indy car is not just built for speed—it also has to be one of the safest cars ever made.

airbox

Sam Hornish, Jr.

THE DRIVER

**RACECAR DRIVER** Dominant, self-reliant, intelligent, emotionally detached, hard-working person with super-fast reflexes. Must be in good physical condition and able to endure extreme heat. Must have the need for speed and the will to win. Experience on 2.5-mile oval track preferred. Can you relax in the midst of life-threatening situations? Apply within.

There is more to being a driver at Indy than just getting behind the wheel and taking off. Before a driver can race in the Indianapolis 500, he or she must pass a rookie test. It is made of four different ten-lap segments. Most drivers who make it this far have already won a championship in another series, such as the Infinity Pro Series (formula cars), Formula Atlantic, or midget or sprint car series.

Champions from all over the world, from all forms of racing, come to test their skills at the Indy 500.

Racecar drivers push their cars—and their bodies—to the limit. Their goal is to drive as fast as they can without crashing. Reaching speeds of 240 miles per hour increases the pull of gravity by four to five times. That means that a 170-pound man will feel as if he weighs 680 pounds! It is the same amount of force an astronaut feels during take off in a space shuttle. The pull is so strong that the Indy Racing League recommends that an Indy 500 driver should use the HANS (Head And Neck System) safety device.

*HANS device*

The helmet has a built-in straw for drinking during the long, hot race. A two-way radio inside the helmet keeps the driver in constant contact with his or her crews.

# WILBUR SHAW: FACING THE FEAR

After his first Indy 500 in 1927, Wilbur Shaw told people, "I felt I had been sucked into a hundred-mile-an-hour tornado. I was never so scared in my life." Scared or not, Wilbur Shaw went on to win the Indy 500 three times!

The driver has to be physically and mentally fit. Most drivers work out every day and keep themselves on special diets. At rest a driver has a normal heart rate of about 60 beats per minute. But while the driver is racing, his or her heart rate may reach 170 to 190 beats per minute—for three to four hours! This is similar to the heart rate of a marathon runner.

The physical needs of a driver include his or her clothing. The drivers wear fireproof long underwear made of Nomex®. Over the Nomex® they wear a quilted jumpsuit, which is also fireproof. Drivers wear thick gloves and a ski-mask-like hood, both made of Nomex®. Then they strap on a helmet and are belted into the cockpit, where the temperatures can reach 120 to 150 degrees Fahrenheit. By the time the checkered flag drops to end the race, a driver will lose six percent of his or her total body weight due to dehydration. For a 170-pound man, that is about 10 pounds of sweat!

*NOMEX® ski mask*

*Jeff Ward gets a little hep from his pit crew.*

Contrary to some people's beliefs, the race driver does not have a "death wish." He or she must be mentally and emotionally stable. A driver must remain calm during life-threatening situations. Racing can be dangerous, so drivers must have a clear mind and logical thinking in order to survive. Like most champions, drivers are usually competitive, assertive, persistent, and very intelligent.

# WOMEN DRIVERS

*Janet Guthrie*

*Lyn St. James*

![Sarah Fisher]

*Sarah Fisher*

For years, the "women of Indy" were the wives of the drivers and crewmembers. In 1977, **Janet Guthrie** changed that. She became the first woman to qualify for the Indianapolis 500. **Lyn St. James** followed in her tire prints in 1992, finishing eleventh in her first year and earning the title of Rookie of the Year. She raced in every Indy 500 from 1992 to 1997. In 2000, **Sarah Fisher** qualified and in May 2002, she became the fastest female qualifier at Indy, with a four-lap average speed of more than 229 miles per hour!

Today, more girls than ever are soapbox derby competitors, quarter midget racers, junior dragsters, and go-kart racers. As these girls explore the training grounds of auto racing, it is likely that more women will qualify for the world's greatest race— the Indianapolis 500.

*Quarter midget racer*

# HOW CAN DRIVERS AFFORD TO RACE?

It takes a lot of money to run an Indy-style car. The race teams rely on sponsors. The sponsors pay to have their product's name on the cars, on driver's suits, on team uniforms, and on transporters.

The cost of an Indy-style car can be more than $300,000. Each driver needs at least two. The wheels of an Indy-style car cost $2,000 apiece. A team needs about ten sets of wheels for each car. Most cars need six engines to get through the month, at a cost of $125,000 each. Even the steering wheel costs $60,000! Transporters get the cars to the races. These big rigs can cost close to $400,000.

How much does it cost to run a racecar in the Indy 500?

**One** driver in **one** car for **one** month costs about **1 million to 1.5 million dollars!**

*transporter*

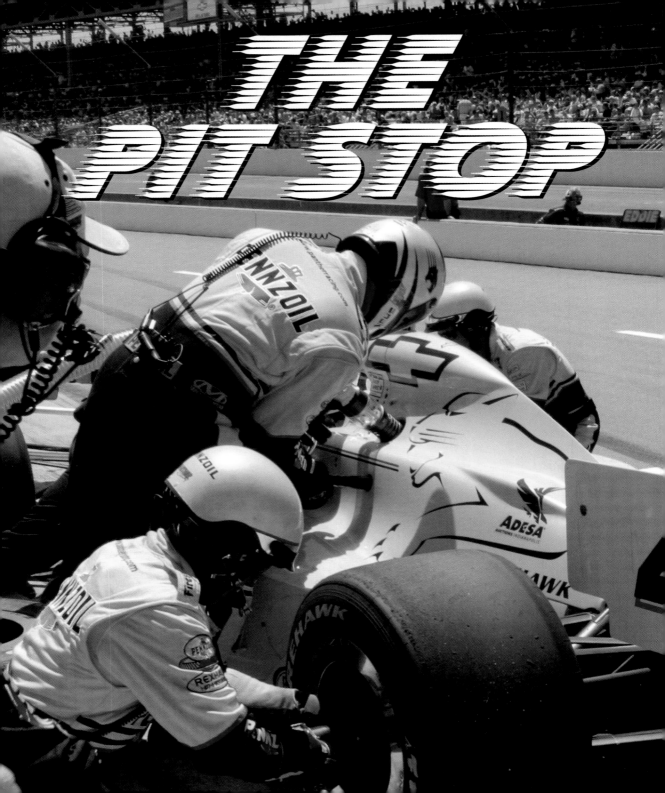

# THE PIT STOP

The Indy 500 race is not only on the track—it is also in the pits. The pits are located beside the front straightaway of the track. Each driver is assigned a pit area. During the race, the mechanics, tires, spare

*tire swap in the pits*

parts, and fuel (methanol) are kept in the pits.

The crew chief watches from behind the pit wall. He talks with the driver by using a two-way radio. In the first Indy 500 in 1911, a riding mechanic rode with the driver.

The cars zip into the pits to refuel, change tires, and make repairs. Teams strive to complete their pit stop in less than eleven seconds. Each team is allowed to have six men over the pit wall to work on the car: four men for tires, one for fuel, and one for the air jack that lifts the car up.

*Sam Hornish, Jr. takes a pit stop.*

# PIT STOP SEQUENCE:
## BUDDY RICE, MAY 30, 2004

**1** Pit crew members signals driver in. Tires and air wrench are in place.

**2** The car pulls into the pits. The air jack man scrambles over the wall and inserts an air hose in a fitting at the top of the car. The compressed air pressurizes the jacks to lift the car up off the ground.

**3** He then inserts a vent in the top of the fuel cell to let the air escape, allowing the gas to go in faster.

**4** Meanwhile, the fueler puts the fuel hose into an opening called a "buckeye."

**5** While the fuel flows, the four tire men sprint to their stations. The wail of impact wrenches pierces the air as they spin the one and only lug nut off each wheel.

**6** Crewmembers behind the wall take away the old wheels and hand over new ones.

**7** Air wrenches are reversed and the new wheels are tightened into place.

**8** Two tire men check the side-pod vents for obstructions while the other two check the wings.

**9** The fueler disconnects the hose and the fuel cell automatically seals itself. Hoses are handed to the crew back over the wall.

**10** The air jack man releases the jack, and the car falls to the ground.

**11** Crewmembers stand behind the car, ready to give it a push if it stalls.

**12** One crewmember by the outside front tire sees all is clear and signals the driver to GO-GO-GO!

*The driver—and his newly tired and fueled car—hit the track and rejoin the race. All in less than twelve seconds!*

The most successful pit crew of the Indy 500 is the Penske racing team. To stay in tune with each other, the Penske team practices several times a month, year-round. Through the years, the team has earned 13 wins and 12 pole positions, more than any other team in history. The Penske team dominated the 500 five times, winning the pole position and the race. Out of the eighteen different men who drove for Penske, nine of them became Indianapolis 500 winners.

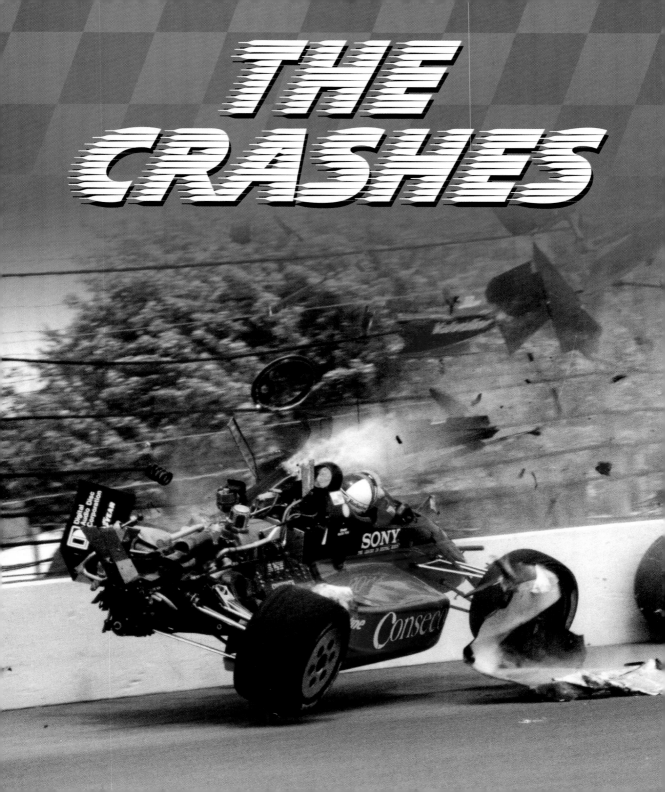

# THE CRASHES

How do so many drivers walk away from 200-mph crashes? Indy-style cars are made to be safe at top speeds. The bodywork absorbs the impact of the crash before it gets to the driver. Parts of the car break off on impact. The driver's feet are protected because they are located behind the front wheels of the car. A six-point safety harness holds the driver tightly inside the cockpit. It has a quick-release buckle to allow him or her to escape quickly. The HANS (head and neck system) fastened to the helmet keeps the driver's head from shooting forward in a sudden stop, reducing neck injuries. And the driver's flame-resistant clothing just might come in handy if the car bursts into flames.

*Johnny Rutherford, 1988*

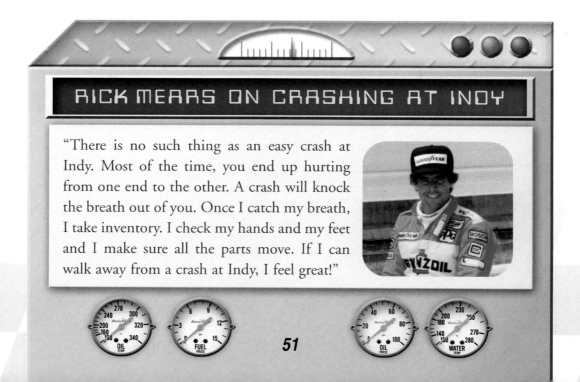

## RICK MEARS ON CRASHING AT INDY

"There is no such thing as an easy crash at Indy. Most of the time, you end up hurting from one end to the other. A crash will knock the breath out of you. Once I catch my breath, I take inventory. I check my hands and my feet and I make sure all the parts move. If I can walk away from a crash at Indy, I feel great!"

# INSIDE AN INDY CRASH

The Indy car driver straps his helmet into place and pulls on his fireproof gloves. He lowers himself into the cockpit of his sleek racing machine. It is qualifying day at the Indianapolis 500 and winning the pole position would be a dream come true. His job is to find the fastest way around the two and a half mile oval, for four consecutive laps. A crewmember buckles up his safety harness. The driver pops the steering wheel into place. The starter is engaged, and the engine roars. The driver slaps the car into gear and cruises down the pit lane.

On the warm-up lap, the driver tests his car. He listens for any sounds of trouble. He feels every little movement and every little bump through the seat of his pants. To warm up the tires, he weaves back and forth on the track. The car feels good! All systems are go. It's time to bring the car up to speed.

He completes the first lap going full speed without needing to brake. The engine is screaming as the car rockets down the straightaway in front of the grandstand, reaching a speed of more than 200 miles per hour.

Once again, he soars through the first turn. As he enters the second turn, a sudden gust of wind pushes the car off the racing line. The rear of the car loses its grip, causing it

*A.J. Foyt IV hits the wall.*

to drift and veer toward the wall. The driver knows the car has passed the point of no return. This spin can't be saved! The wall is coming at him—and then it's gone. He's headed for the wall again—and then it's gone. He knows he has no choice but to go along for the ride—a wild ride. He is on a rollercoaster without tracks, launched into the unknown.

With no hope of avoiding the crash, the driver realizes it's time for "turtle mode." He lets go of the steering wheel and pulls his arms to his sides. He knows that if he hangs onto the steering wheel, the impact of the crash could shatter his wrists. He puts his head down and closes his eyes.

Spectators see the car slam into the wall while skidding down the track backwards. The sound of metal scraping the concrete barrier pierces the air. The tires are screeching, and the air smells of burning rubber. The car is breaking into pieces around the driver. Sheet metal drags down the track behind the crumbled car. Then suddenly the driver feels as if he were shot out of a cannon into a concrete wall. His head shakes back and forth inside his helmet, like a clapper inside a ringing bell. Everything goes black. The wall has delivered the knockout punch.

Seconds later, he opens his eyes. The force of the impact is so great that he cannot move, he cannot speak, and he can hardly breathe. He tries to force air down into his lungs, but heaviness settles on his chest and his lungs tighten. The car finally stops. Although his vision is blurred, he takes inventory of all his body parts. He wiggles his hands and feet to make certain they move.

*Johnny Rutherford, 1988*

The safety crew is already at his side. With fire extinguishers ready for action, they unbuckle the safety harness and pull the stunned driver out of the car. The driver is helped into the ambulance to be taken to the trackside hospital. He must see the doctor before he can be released to get back into the race in his back-up car.

He knows that soon he will be hurting all over, but for the moment, he feels great. He knows he is a lucky man. He has survived a crash at the Indianapolis 500.

## KENNY BRACK CRASHES IN 1999

Winner of the 1999 Indy 500, Kenny Brack survived one of the worst crashes in Indy car history in 2003 at the Texas Motor Speedway. The accident recorded 200 G-forces, meaning he felt the pressure of 200 times his own body weight on impact. "At the end of the crash," says Brack, "everything broke off the car, absorbing the impact. But my cockpit was intact. Nothing penetrated it. It probably saved my life. My crash was a testament to how safe these cars are."

# THE FLAGS

The checkered flag has been waved at the Indy 500 since the first race in 1911. Since then, other flags have been added to let the drivers know about the condition of the track and the flow of the race. The flags are used during practice, qualifying, and the race itself, to keep the race as safe as possible and to enforce regulations. Even with all the high-tech radios, computers, and spotters, the flags are a good way to "talk" to the drivers during the noisy racing action. The flags tell the drivers important things, like "Slow down," "Stop! The track is unsafe!" or "One lap to go!" The checkered flag means "The End!"

*The checkered flags mark the end of the race.*

## LAPS AND LAPTOPS

Computers have invaded the world of Indy cars. Engineer Walter Preston of Team Rahal says, "Laptops and flat screens—you can't live without them anymore. It's a total video game." The drivers and crews rely on the Pi data retrieving system, hidden in the car's sidepod. It gathers information through sensors on the cars and transmitters on the track. The Pi box is "the brains" of the racecar. It records and calculates everything from fuel mileage, G forces, lap time, lap speed, corner speeds, oil temperatures, tire pressures, gear ratios, ride height, and much, much more. It "talks" to the driver through an LED (Light Emitting Diodes) display on the steering wheel. The pit crew and the driver use the data to make decisions and adjustments about the car and their race strategy.

### GREEN
## Start! Go!
This flag is used to start the race or to restart the race after a yellow or red flag.

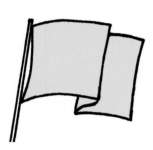

### YELLOW
## Caution!
Conditions are unsafe. Slow down and keep your position. Passing is not allowed while the yellow flag is out. Cars can bunch up single-file. The yellow flag comes out for debris on the track, an oil spill, or an accident. Drivers must yield to track safety vehicles.

### BLACK
## Into the pits!
The driver who gets the black flag must take his car into the pits immediately.

## BLUE WITH DIAGONAL ORANGE STRIPE
### Let them pass!
The slower cars must allow the faster cars to pass.

## RED
### Stop!
The race is stopped because it is unsafe to continue racing.

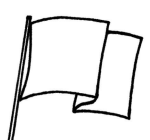

## WHITE
### One lap left!
This flag is waved when the leader has only one lap left of his 500-mile race.

## BLACK-AND-WHITE CHECKERED
### The race is over!
The first car shown the black-and-white checkered flag is the winner.

# SO, YOU WANT TO BE AN INDY DRIVER . . .

Did you know that you can start your racing career as early as age five? Racing go-karts is a great training ground for future Indy car drivers. Karting is offered on dirt tracks, paved tracks, oval tracks, or road courses. Purchasing a kart of your own costs about $2,000 to $5,000. Karting schools offer rentals from $25.00 to $500.00. "The younger you start, the better. The best way to get ready to drive bigger cars is to start with go-karts," says former go-kart racer and 2004 Indy 500 Winner Buddy Rice. Some series available to 15- to 20-year-olds moving through the ranks are the Formula Ford, Formula Barber Dodge, Formula Mazda, and the Formula BMW. The steppingstone to the Indy Racing League is the Infinity Pro Series. Once you get there, you could be just one step away from racing at Indy!

BUDDY RICE

*2004 Indy 500 Winner*

"Buy a kart, invest in tires and gas, and go racing!"

# *ACKNOWLEDGMENTS*

I want to thank many special people for helping make this book possible: my friend John Anderson, for sharing his knowledge and expertise in the field of auto racing; Jim Trueman, Mike Curb, and Patrick Kehoe for believing in my husband, Ed Pimm, and helping to make his dream of racing in the Indy 500 come true; Rick Mears, Bobby Rahal, Ed Pimm, Mario Andretti, Kenny Brack, Buddy Rice, and Lyn St. James for sharing their memories and stories with me. You've made me discover that auto racing is not for the faint of heart. You are true warriors! Thanks, too, to Rahal Letterman Racing for all their help, especially Bill VandeSandt, Linda Lett, Donna Filson, Walter Preston, and Scott Roembke.

Heartfelt thanks also go to Stephanie Greene for being the best cheerleader a writer ever had, to my critique group in Columbus, Ohio—Erin MacLellan, Carol Ottolenghi, Andrea Pelleschi, and Kristi Lewis—and to my mentor, editor, and friend, Tanya Dean, for believing in me and for believing in this book.

Most of all, I'd like to thank my husband, Ed Pimm, for sharing his love of auto racing and showing me the way to follow your dreams, no matter how far-fetched they may seem.

*-NRP*

# BIBLIOGRAPHY

Anderson, John. Senior Manager of Technology for Champ Cars, Formerly Crew Chief and Team Manager for many Indy 500 Race Teams. Interview: August 2002.

Andretti, Mario. 1969 Indianapolis 500 Winner; Championship Auto Racing Team Owner. Interview: September 2002.

Brack, Kenny. 1999 Indianapolis 500 Winner and driver for Team Rahal. Interview: April 2004.

Carnegie, Tom. *Indy 500—More Than a Race*. Tokyo, Japan: McGraw-Hill Book Company, [n.d.].

Dregni, Michael. *The Indianapolis 500*. Minneapolis, Minnesota: Capstone Press, 1994

Maynard, Chris. Racing Cars. London, England: Frank Watts, 1999.

Mears, Rick. Four-time Indianapolis 500 Winner: 1979, 1984, 1988, and 1991. Consultant for Team Penske. August 2003.

Popely, Rick with Spencer Riggs. *Indianapolis 500 Chronicle*. Lincolnwood, Illinois: Publications International, Ltd. 1998.

Preston, Walter. Race engineer for Team Rahal, Formula Atlantic. Interview: April 2004.

Rahal, Bobby. 1986 Indianapolis 500 Winner; Team owner: Indy Racing League, Formula Atlantic Team, Championship Auto Racing Team. Interview: September 2003.

Rice, Buddy. Driver in 2003 Indianapolis 500 for Team Rahal. Interview: April 2004.

Rubel, David. *How to Drive an Indy Race Car*. Santa Fe, New Mexico: Agincourt Press, 1992.

Savage, Jeff. *Racing Cars*. Minneapolis, Minnesota: Capstone Press, 1961.

Schwartz, Chris. Director of Marketing and Communications for Penske Racing. Interview: January 2004.

St. James, Lyn. 1992 Rookie of the Year at Indy. Second woman to qualify for the Indianapolis 500. Interview: January 2004.

Taylor, Rich. *Indy: Seventy-Five Years of Racing's Greatest Spectacle*. New York, New York: St. Martin's Press, 1991.

Weber, Bruce. *The Indianapolis 500*. Mankato, Minnesota: Creative Education, Inc., 1990.

Wukovits, John F. *The Composite Guide to Auto Racing*. Philadelphia, Pennsylvania: Chelsea House Publishers, 1999.

# BIBLIOGRAPHY

**http://brickyard.com/500/**

The official website for the Indianapolis 500 Hall of Fame Museum. They have schedules, tickets, photos, and more.

**http://www.indy500.com/stats/**

Contains driver biographies, driver statistics, qualifying records, race winners, race, and all-time statistics. You can even purchase photographs of your favorite drivers.

**http://www.indyracing.com/indycar/**

Contains Indy Racing Series results. You can sign up for an e-newsletter, shop at a fan store, take a virtual lap around a racetrack, or check the schedule of your favorite drivers' appearances.

**http://lynstjames.com**

Information about the Lyn St. James Foundation, a program that mentors young females who want to race.

**http://skipbarber.com**

All about a school that teaches young people the art and craft of racecar driving. Also at **www.skipbarber.com/karting**, you can find out how to go from go-karts to Skip Barber school.

**http://worldkarting.com**

A great site for kids interested in the world of go-kart racing.

*Indianapolis Motor Speedway pagoda*

# GLOSSARY

**aerodynamics**   the science that deals with the effects of the car moving through air.

**airflow**   the movement of air around the chassis of a racecar.

**bite**   the adhesion of a tire to the track's surface.

**carbon fiber**   a high-tech material made of fibers woven and mixed with glues. It can be formed into any shape, and then heated to make a material harder than steel.

**cockpit**   the place in the car where a driver sits.

**downforce**   the force that presses the car to the ground, produced by air flowing under and over the moving car.

**fuel cell**   a container that holds methanol in a racecar, similar to a gas tank in a passenger car.

**ground effects**   the downforce created by both the low pressure area between the underbody and the ground and the front and rear wings.

**horsepower**   a unit for measuring an engine's power, originally based on the amount of effort a number of horses exert as they pull a load.

**lap**   a single complete circuit of a racetrack.

**methanol**   pure methyl alcohol that is used as fuel in all Indy Racing League IndyCar Series cars.

**Nomex®**   the trade name for DuPont's fire-resistant fabric that is used to make protective clothing.

**pits**   the place beside the racetrack where crews add fuel, change tires, or make repairs during a race.

**pole position**   the position on the inside of the first row at the beginning of a race, usually awarded to the fastest car during qualifying races.

**side pod**   bodywork on the side of the car that covers the radiators and engine exhaust. It aids in engine cooling, aerodynamics, and protection of the driver during a side impact.

**slicks**   smooth tires used for racing on dry surfaces.

**splash-and-go**   a pit stop in which the driver stops only for fuel.

**sponsor**   a company or individual who provides the financial support for a race team.

**time trials**   the four laps that the drivers take alone on the track to determine who qualifies for the Indianapolis 500. The thirty-three fastest four-lap averages qualify.

**transporter**   a huge truck that carries the racecar and supplies to the races.

**Venturi**   a narrow tunnel under the side pod, shaped like an inverted wing. Air through the tunnel creates low pressure or a suction effect, which holds the car to the track.